God

Justice

Love

Beauty

God
Justice
Love
Beauty

FOUR LITTLE DIALOGUES

JEAN-LUC NANCY

TRANSLATED BY SARAH CLIFT

FORDHAM UNIVERSITY PRESS ✦ *New York*

This work was originally published in French as *Dieu, La justice, L'amour, La beauté: Quatre petites conférences*, © Bayard Éditions 2009.

This work has been published with the assistance of the National Center for the Book—French Ministry of Culture.

Ouvrage publié avec le soutien du Centre national du livre—ministère français chargé de la culture.

Nancy, Jean-Luc.
   [Dieu, la justice, l'amour, la beauté. English]
   God, justice, love, beauty : four little dialogues / Jean-Luc Nancy ; translated by Sarah Clift.
      p. cm.
   Includes bibliographical references.
   ISBN 978-0-8232-3425-7 (cloth : alk. paper)
   ISBN 978-0-8232-3426-4 (pbk.)
   1. God.   2. Justice (Philosophy)   3. Love.   4. Aesthetics.   I. Title.
B2430.N363D5413   2011
194—dc22

                                  2011010768

Printed in the United States of America
18 17 16   5 4 3 2
First edition

Contents

Author's Note

The following texts are transcriptions of talks given at Montreuil's Center for the Dramatic Arts as part of a series entitled "Little Dialogues." Organized by Gilberte Tsaï, Director of the Center, the series was designed to address children. The transcriptions were done with care and precision, and I would like to express my gratitude here for this work. Nonetheless, a transcription can never capture the rhythm or the tones, to say nothing of the whole pragmatic context, of a talk, which themselves convey a great deal of information. As we well know, "communication" is inseparable from its event. This is all the more true of talks addressed to children and of the exchanges that followed. The children, both boys and girls, were between six and twelve years of age. They were extremely attentive during my talks, and as you will see, they were not without questions at the end. What these encounters could have meant for them, I cannot say, but for me, they were risky endeavors.

I only know that for me, the aim of the talks was not to popularize the issues, nor was it to indulge in a kind of "feat" of skill regarding my treatment of them. It was a matter of once again finding myself in contact with thinking in the very process of its awakening—for, whatever the forms or degrees of its elaboration, thinking is always essentially in this state, or better, in this movement. It is not the case, then, that an elderly thinker is placing himself within reach of children here: rather, within him a contact with this awakening is searching for itself, an awakening without which there would be no thinking [*il n'y aurait de penser*] (I indeed used the infinitive form of the verb).

God

Translated by Pascale-Anne Brault and Michael Naas

It is not without trepidation that I am allowing this transcription to be published. It should thus only be read, it seems to me, in an attempt to hear something of its actual "articulation." This was also the result of difficulties inherent in the theme I had chosen. I had selected it because of certain philosophical interests I have tried to develop in the course of a work I have elsewhere called a "deconstruction of Christianity." But since it was out of the question to introduce this theme or this concept as such, it was necessary for me to proceed without offending the religious convictions of the children but also without giving in to any simplification (it being the case that for me "atheism" and "theism" are but two symmetrical and connected postulations, both based in the same metaphysical presuppositions with regard to being). A transposition into writing of something that was not at all a text and that was the result of a very particular form of address risks at each step erasing both the difficulties encountered and the precautions taken. I can do nothing but warn the reader of this here at the outset.

*Y*es, I am going to speak to you about god, but first I am going to speak to you about heaven [*ciel*]. You know why, of course. If god exists, he is in heaven.

The word *ciel* is a rather odd word in the French language because it has two plurals, which some of you children may know. There is the plural *cieux*, which you probably know, and then another plural, *ciels*, which many of you probably don't know because it is used only in reference to painting. One speaks of the *ciels*, of the skies, of a painter, the *ciels* of Vermeer, for example.

Cieux is an exclusively religious word. One says "*dans les cieux*"—that is, "in the heavens" or "in heaven." It is a word familiar to those in the Christian tradition or with a Christian background. One says, for example, "Hosanna in the highest heaven [*des cieux*]." *Hosanna* is a Hebrew word that comes from the religious vocabulary of Judaism.

The plural *cieux*, which, again, has its origin in an exclusively religious vocabulary, has to do with the fact that, in antiquity, it was thought that there were many *cieux*, many heavens. It was thought that the *ciel* was a sphere, that what we see as the *ciel* was a sphere surrounding the earth, and that there was a set of concentric spheres one inside the other.

There are different versions of this belief, but according to the best known there were seven heavens—the number seven having always had a sacred value—with the seventh heaven being the highest. Sometimes still today when we want to say that we are absolutely delighted or ecstatic we speak of being in "seventh heaven."

There are thus many heavens [*cieux*], as if to indicate the extreme or utmost nature of the highest heaven, the highest heavenly region. And this plural exists in French because the French comes from Latin, which comes from the Greek, which comes from the Hebrew of the Bible. The same plural also exists in the Arabic of the Koran.

As for the other *ciels*, those of painting, this refers to the way in which a painter represents the *ciel*, that is, the sky. But why is there a plural unique to painting? No doubt because the *ciel* is a dimension or a particular element of our vision, of our perception of the world, and of our way of being in the world.

There is the earth, there is what we see on the horizon, and then there is what is above. The sky [*ciel*] appears far away, at a distance, elevated, transparent, translucid, almost immaterial. We might say that the sky is on the side of the open. It is the dimension of opening. When we look at the earth before us, on the other hand, everything is always closed, everything stops at a certain distance. We will come back later to what is involved in this dimension of the *ciel*, to the place of the *ciel* in our experience, and in relation to the role it plays in religious traditions.

But for now, let's ask about what's in heaven [*le ciel*]. Already I am speaking the language of religion, or at least of the three great so-called monotheistic religions, that is, those religions with a single god, the three great religions that predominate in the West. Later on I will say just a word or two about those religions that are not monotheistic.

"In heaven" [*"au ciel"*] is also a phrase that belongs to religious language. It is often said in religion that those who have died or the souls of those who have died are "in heaven." It is also sometimes said that angels are "in heaven." I won't be speaking to you today about angels, however, or about the souls of the dead, though we can discuss this later if you want. Finally, it is also said that god is "in heaven."

So let's just note this: "in heaven" [*"au ciel"*] has to do with god, with the realm of god, with what is divine. Indeed the divine is the heavenly, the celestial [*céleste*]. The adjective *céleste*—heavenly—is also a word that is more or less restricted to a religious vocabulary, though it also sometimes appears in a certain poetic language. *Céleste* is also a first name, a girl's name, with the diminutive *Célestine* and the masculine *Célestin*. Perhaps there are some Célestes, Célestines, or Célestins here in the audience, though I myself have yet to meet anyone with this name.

The heavenly is the dimension of the divine, the divine as what is elevated, lifted up above the earth, and also, as a result, so elevated and so immaterial that it is infinitely distant. Finally, heaven [*le ciel*], like the seventh heaven of antiquity or the seventh heaven in the Koran, is always the highest, the most elevated. It is the place of the one who is called in the Bible "the Most High," the one who is absolutely high.

Now, this is not unique to the three great Western monotheisms. There are many religions in which god or the gods bear the name of height. To give just one example: the main god of the Iroquois Indians, at least in their traditional culture, is called or used to be called "Oki," which means "the one on high." There are many other religions like this, in many other cultures. I know I have probably not yet said anything that surprises you. Heaven [*le ciel*] is divine and, reciprocally, the divine, which has to do with god, is celestial.

Today, in the twenty-first century, what is up there in the sky, in the heavens [*le ciel*]? We all know quite well what's up there. There is a whole bunch of things that are not at all gods. There are clouds, airplanes, and, further away, satellites and spacecraft; there are all the other planets of the solar system; there are all the other systems beyond our solar system, and then a very large number of other systems called galaxies. It's hard to get an idea of the magnitude here, but I know that with a telescope—you may have heard of the Hubble telescope, which is currently in orbit and was just recently repaired with considerable effort—one can observe what is very very far away, I don't know exactly how far, but it's at an enormous distance. You know that we measure these things in light years, that is, the distance that light, or a photon of light, which travels at 186,000 miles per second, can travel in a year.

As far as we can see, there are things, but there is no god; no telescope has ever seen god. You will, of course, say that this is to be expected because you all have some sense, whether you are believers or not, whether you come from a religious family or not, that god is not visible. So it's perfectly to be expected that we don't see him. But that also means that heaven [*le ciel*], in the religious sense of the term, is not the heavens [*le ciel*] above, what we see with our eyes or through a telescope. You know that some time back we sent to Mars a little space probe, which could be seen trekking across the surface of the planet. Someday soon we may be able to send something even further away. It's thus not the same *ciel*.

When religions speak of heaven [*le ciel*] and of the height of the heavenly [*céleste*], of the Most High, they are not speaking of what is up above. In fact, our sky or our heavens [*le ciel*] are not above, either, because they are also below. All you have to do is dig through to the other side of the earth to see the heavens above the Australians, who are below us, as you know, because they are in the southern hemisphere, in the land "down under," as we say.

So the heaven [*le ciel*] of religions means something else, *le ciel*, or *les cieux*, the celestial, the most high. It means a place very different from the world as a whole. In this sense, we have to say that the sky or heavens [*le ciel*] of airplanes, spacecraft, and galaxies, the heavens of the astronomers, are a part of the world. They are part of the world, part of what is called, as you know, the universe.

This religious idea of heaven [*le ciel*] refers not to something in the world, something higher than everything else, nor to another world, a world that would be above the world, because that would just be the same thing. It designates, we might say, a place different from the world as a whole. But a place different from the world as a whole means a place that is different from all places. That, then, means a place that is not a place. Playing a bit with the French word *endroit*, which, as a noun, means *place*, and, as an adverb, *on the right side*, I would say that it's a place that is not a place, not even a faraway place, but not an *envers* or flipside either. It is not a place in the world, but it's also not as if we were going to the other side of the world, as if we were looking at another side or face of the world. As if this other side or face were god, as if the face of god were on the backside of the world, like the backside or hidden face of the moon.

You know, perhaps, that we always see the same side or face of the moon because of the way it turns around the earth and the way the earth turns on itself. Only spacecraft circling the moon have been able to photograph the other side. But it's still another side, whereas in the case of the world, the world in its totality, the universe in its complete totality, assuming we could get to the end of it in every direction, there is no other side, by definition. Since space ends at that point . . . there are no other spaces, places, or locations. There is no place outside the world.

So, when we say heaven [*le ciel*], or the divine as what is in heaven, we are talking about something that would be nowhere, in no place, and at the same time, as a result, everywhere. Something, assuming we can say "something," or "someone," who would be nowhere and everywhere.

And since being nowhere and everywhere means, strictly speaking, nothing when we are talking about the things of the world, this means that the heavenly or the divine designates something that is nothing. We really don't have any other way of saying this. Something that is not a thing, neither a thing nor a person, in the sense that a person is a thing. For a person is there just as much as this glass is. So we are talking about something with another manner or way of being than the being of all things and all persons.

To give you an analogy, it's a bit like air, which is more or less everywhere and nowhere, though this isn't completely true because there are places where there is no air, where matter is so dense that a molecule of air cannot penetrate. But if you find the analogy at all helpful, you can use it, so long as you remember that air itself is nonetheless something.

This something or someone that would not be outside the world, because there is no outside of the world, but that would be something other than the world as a whole, other than all things, is nowhere, neither within nor elsewhere, and it is at the same time present everywhere but in a very particular mode of presence—and that's what religions call god, or the gods.

What can we say about god or the gods if we don't start with religion, if we don't place ourselves in a religion that says "god goes by this name and has these characteristics"? For instance, some say that god goes by a name that one is not allowed to pronounce. This is the Jewish god: four letters that must not be pronounced. Or else he is simply called god—we will return to this—and that's the Christian god, along with the question of Jesus Christ, which we can also return to later. Or else god is called Allah, the god of Islam. Or else he goes by many different names in all those religions where there are many gods, in what are called polytheistic religions. In these cases, the gods have proper names. For example, in the Shinto religion of Japan there are millions of gods. The way in which god or the divine is everywhere can be seen there in the way gods are everywhere, on every corner and in every place. In the streets of Japan you see statues of gods or of divine beings more or less everywhere.

But I'm not going to get into this difference between polytheistic religions, those religions with many gods, and monotheistic ones, religions with a single god, because this would be much too long and complicated. For our purposes we can assume that god or the gods play the same role or have the same function more or less everywhere, at least up to a certain point, and that we can try to think what this means in the same way.

From here on, I'm going to stay within the framework of our Western, Mediterranean, European culture, and thus within the framework of the three religions with a single god, within the three monotheisms, and these are the Jewish religion, the Christian religion, and Islam. And I am going to ignore all the internal differences, the internal divisions, within each of these religions.

Common to this group of religions is the notion that there is only one god. And in each of these religions god is called "god." Notice here that *god* is a rather peculiar name: *god* is a common name—"a god," or "the gods" in polytheistic religions with many gods, for example, in the Greek and Roman religions of Western antiquity. One thus spoke of "the gods," but no god was called "god." Zeus, for example, was a god, and, even before Greece, the Egyptian Osiris was a god and Isis a goddess. But none of these gods was called "god."

When we use the name *god* as the name of the one god, we are doing something rather unique, since we are saying that there is a divine, heavenly being who goes by the name of all divine beings. It is as if we were to say that the name of a "poplar" tree is simply *tree*. As a result, the name *god* perhaps does not name someone, it is not the proper name of someone, but names the divine as such, the divine as a unity or single thing, as if it were a person. And this is the case, let me say in passing, of *dieu* in the French language, as well as for all European languages, and it is also the case for *Allah*, which is the name of the god of Islam. But *Allah* is a transformation of a very old common name or noun of Semitic origin, namely, the word *el*, meaning "god." This language is the origin of a group of common languages that then gave rise both to Hebrew and to Arabic and other languages. Already in very ancient civilizations, then, there was a supreme god who was called precisely *el*, "god," and *Allah* is a transformation of *el*.

But now we come to the key question: Does god exist? I hope you have already understood that this question is perhaps not the right one. Asking whether god exists in this way would be a bit like asking whether Célestin Dupont exists. Is there someone named Célestin Dupont? I could look on the Internet, I could look at all existing names, and I either will or will not find a Célestin Dupont.

But to ask whether god exists is to ask the question of whether there is, somewhere, a someone or a something that would answer to the name of god.

When religion says that god exists, it perhaps never says exactly that. But let's say that the religious answer more or less comes down to affirming: "Yes, god exists." If that is the case, let me assure you that among all religious people, and not simply among theologians, that is, scholars who study various aspects of religion, but among priests, imams, or rabbis, those who are not necessarily scholars but who are concerned with what religion represents and with the relationship between religion and the people of a particular religious community, there are very few people today who would say: "Yes, god exists, and he is in fact right up there, in the seventh heaven, all you have to do is go up there and you will see him. He has a face with a long beard . . ." A Muslim especially will not say that. It is perhaps in Islam that there is the most acute sense that god looks like nothing, absolutely nothing. This is repeated throughout the Koran.

More generally, what religion says in this form can be understood, I think, even outside religion. I myself, for example, am speaking to you completely outside any religion. We can thus understand these things in a different way. Finally, in speaking of god, we are speaking of this name that is like a proper name and yet is not a proper name since it does not name someone who would be somewhere, someone who would have certain characteristics proper to him or her, like those of Célestin Dupont. But god names the possibility that there exists for us collectively, as well as for each of us singularly and individually, a relationship with this nowhere and everywhere. In other words, god, or the divine, or the celestial, would name the fact that I am in relation not with something but with the fact that I am not limited to all those relations I have with all the things of the world, or even with all the beings of the world. It suggests that there is something else, which I will here call "the opening," something that makes me be, that makes us be as humans open to something more than being in the world, more than being able to take things up, manipulate them, eat them, get around in the world, send space probes to Mars, look at galaxies through telescopes, and so on. It suggests that there is all this but also something else.

What is this something else? We have some idea of this other thing, and perhaps more than an idea, a feeling, through the fact, for example, that we know what it is to feel great joy or great sadness, what it is to feel love or, I won't say hate, but at least a feeling that is very far from love. When I have such feelings or moods I sense that there is something immense, infinite, which I cannot simply locate somewhere. For when I feel joy or sadness, love or hatred, force or weakness, there is in all this something that infinitely exceeds what I am, my person, my personality, my means, my location, my way of being someone in a particular place in the world. In all this there is some kind of opening. Now, the god of the three monotheistic religions, and all the other gods as well, god himself, represents nothing other than this.

To take the three monotheistic religions in their historical order, what is the Jewish god? We might say that the Jewish god is the Father, but perhaps that's not the best image. The Jewish god is essentially the Just One. He is Justice, the Judge, not in the sense of the one who brings justice but as the one who appreciates the just or right measure of each and every one. In the Bible, he is the god who "trieth the hearts and minds" (Psalm 7:9). But that does not mean he's a super-cop who looks into and knows what is deep within your heart. It means that each one, with his own heart, that is, with what each is most profoundly, most personally, has a measure, an absolute measure in himself and for himself of justice. I am myself, and each is him or herself; and this way of being absolutely oneself, of having for oneself a unique and singular measure, one that distinguishes each absolutely from all others, but that can only be put into action in one's relationship with all the others, that is what is meant by the justice of god.

The Christian god is Love. This is a phrase from what is called the New Testament: "god is Love." It means that god is not someone but is, instead, love. "Love" is a unique relationship between someone and someone else, a relation that goes far beyond everything else. It is not a relationship of pleasure, of getting along, of liking one another—"I like you, you like me." It is the fact of recognizing in the other what is absolutely unique about them. This is actually the way parents love their children. They don't love them because they are beautiful, kind, charming, and so on, since when they come into the world they are not yet any of these things.

The god of Islam is the god who is called the Merciful at the beginning of each chapter—or *sourate*—of the Koran. The Merciful is the one who acknowledges in each man his shortcomings and frailties, and who gives him the possibility of standing tall and worthy despite his short-comings and frailties.

The Just, Love, the Merciful—that is in the end what heaven is, or the celestial in the sense of the divine. This brings us back to the image of the sky or the heavens, that is, to the fact that, above the earth, there opens a dimension that is no longer even a dimension but the opening, wide open and bottomless. There is nothing to see at the bottom of those heavens, just as there is nothing for our physical eyes to see at the bottom or end of the sky. It's not a question of sending space probes or of looking through tele-scopes. There is nothing to see at the bottom of this sky or this heaven [ciel]. But what has to be seen, or known, or understood, or felt is that there is this dimension of open-ing. At this point, at least for the moment, it matters little whether one is a believer or a nonbeliever. It matters little whether one belongs to one religion or religious commu-nity rather than another, or to none at all. Of course, this does become important later on, and there is much to say about it. But at the point we are at right now, I would say that this doesn't matter. What matters instead is under-standing that what is at stake here is the impossibility of closing this opening. That is, the impossibility of being a human being as one might be a stone, a tree, or perhaps also an animal. I say "perhaps" in order to simplify things, because there are some people who would be unhappy to hear me make such a sharp distinction between human beings and everything else. To be a human being is to be open to infinitely more than simply being a human being.

You are probably going to say to me: "This is a very general idea, and I understand what you are saying here. One can call this idea Love, Justice, Mercy, or the opening." According to Pascal, who was a thinker, philosopher, religious figure, and very learned man of the seventeenth century, "man goes infinitely beyond man." You are going to tell me that these are all just ideas. Why call any of them god? Why have religions used this word *god*? Why even outside of religion is it not so easy to do without naming god in one way or another? Because it is not enough to use abstract names like Love, Joy, Mercy, or Justice in order to name this dimension of opening and of going beyond. It is necessary to be able to address oneself to or to relate to this dimension. Why address oneself to this dimension or establish a connection with it? In order to be faithful to it.

What does it mean to be oneself as much as possible, and thus to be as much a human being as possible? It means nothing other than being faithful to this opening or to this infinite going beyond of the human by the human. It means being faithful to the sky or the heavens, in the sense I've spoken of. This fidelity might look like a fidelity to someone, just as infidelity is usually understood as an infidelity to someone. The religious name of this fidelity is "faith" or *foi*, from the Latin *fides*; this same word and this same notion of fidelity can also be found in the word *confidence*.

Faith is the relationship of fidelity. As a result, as a relation of fidelity to . . . , faith takes the shape of a fidelity to someone, someone who is not of this world, and who as a result is not some person outside the world either, but who is to be understood, as I just said, in terms of this relationship of fidelity. This faith, fidelity, or confidence has, in a certain sense, nothing to do with what is called belief.

In religion, there is belief. When one believes, one says that god does this or that. In Christian belief, for example, which is probably the one most of you know best, it is said that god has a son, Jesus Christ, who was incarnated and who died on the cross to save mankind. And then there is a third person called the Holy Spirit . . . There are so many things that could be said about this. But all that is the content of belief, that is, the way things are presented in a particular religion, the way one explains the reality of god. But belief can always lead to thinking that things are like this.

One imagines a father and a son. How is the father able to have a son when the father is a god and the son is a man? The Christian religion here speaks of a mystery. Islam, on the other hand, says that this simply cannot be, that it runs absolutely contrary to the nature of god, that it is impossible for god to be in many persons, that he is absolutely one, that it is impossible for god to have a human son, and so on.

This huge opposition is in the end an opposition only in the way of presenting things. It has to do with belief. And belief has to do with a way of presenting things. I believe that right now it is nice outside, for example. It's a supposition; I would have to go outside to know whether it's true. If, on the contrary, I say, "I don't know what it's like outside, but I am faithful to the idea that it's nice out. [This is of course absurd!] And so I am going to go out in short sleeves and I won't take a raincoat or an umbrella." Yes, I would be taking a big risk, and that would be rather silly. But that's fidelity. Fidelity does not consist in believing, and thus in supposing, in accordance with what we know, that things will be in conformity with what we believe. Fidelity means not at all knowing about this. When one is faithful to someone, one does not know in the end about this person at all, nor about what he or she will become later on in life. But if one is faithful to him or her, one is faithful without knowing.

Let me stop there. One can say at least that in the name of god and in the name of god as the celestial or the heavenly there is at least the indication of the possibility, perhaps the necessity, of being faithful without any knowledge or even any quasi-knowledge, and thus any belief, of being faithful to what I called the opening, without which we would perhaps not even be human beings, but simply things among other things within a world closed upon itself.

—Montreuil, May 4, 2002

Questions and Answers

Q: You said that in the Jewish religion god is just. But if god is just, why are there children born with handicaps or things like that?

J-LN: Well, you're right. You are asking one of the most important questions in relationship to god, a question that has often been asked since the beginning of modern times. It's a question that has often appeared since the eighteenth century, though it was also raised before that.

Why is there evil? In the three great monotheisms there is a single, common answer. In religious terms, it is said that if god creates man, it is in order to create a free being, one that is left to be or to become what he is. And so if god guaranteed human beings in advance all the conditions of a perfect existence, one that required no questions, then we would obviously not be free.

You are among those who were born handicapped. Two things might be said here. It is possible that certain people seem to be more unjustly treated than others by god or by nature. But this goes hand in hand with the fact that men have been able to invent all sorts of solutions to problems of handicaps and diseases, even if we are very far from solving all these problems. But man is also the one who can allow a handicapped person to realize himself as a person, whether this be by medical means, technical means, or some other.

Justice, in the sense of divine justice, justice for the whole world, does not mean that everything is evenly distributed and that nothing else needs to be done. That

GOD

would be to imagine the creation of the world as a sort of Lego game where there is nothing left to do.

Q: Where does the sky, or where do the heavens, begin?

J-LN: I heard just a little while ago an extraordinary phrase from an astronomer who was here earlier.[1] He said that someone had told him that "The heavens [le ciel] begin right at ground level." This wonderful statement suggests that the sky begins right on the ground. I'm speaking in an imagistic and symbolic way. It means that where the earth ends, the sky or the heavens begin, that is, the dimension of opening begins. At the same time, wherever there is ground, however close to the earth we may be, there is sky.

This question might suggest something else, precisely in relation to painting and to the skies we spoke of earlier in painting. Try to look at the way the great landscape painters, like the Flemish painter Jacob Ruisdael or the English painter John Constable, worked with landscapes. You will see there precisely this relationship between a big sky, often full of clouds, and the earth. It is as if the whole painting were done simply to show this opening of the two, and thus the line that runs between them and keeps them apart [qui les partage].

Q: When you were speaking earlier about the god of the Jews, why is one not allowed to pronounce his name?

J-LN: Because that's the Jewish way of saying things. The Jewish god is the first in the history of monotheisms. All

20

monotheisms in fact have a common source; they all come, according to the account in the Bible, from Abraham; they are all Abrahamic religions. And each subsequent religion recognizes the others as its ancestors. As for the last one, Islam, the Koran speaks of Jesus Christ, of Moses, and of Abraham.

The Jewish god is the first who is presented as singular, as unique. First of all, he is not exactly claimed to be the one and only god for all men, but the one god of the Jews of Israel, the god of Israel.

Like the gods of other religions, then, he has a name, but his particularity resides in the fact that his name, since it is the name of the Most High, is a sacred name, a name different from all other names, and thus it is not to be pronounced.

In the Bible he sometimes goes by the name that we pronounce "Yahweh." It is made up of four letters in Hebrew, and when it is pronounced with the vowels it makes "Yahweh." But there are other places in the Bible where he is called, as I mentioned earlier, *el*, or in the plural *eloïm*, but it's the same thing.

One might say that this is the first step toward the disappearance of the proper name of god, and the replacement of the proper name by a common name, which then itself becomes a proper name.

Q: Why and how does god exist?

J-LN: Oh boy.

(*Laughter.*)

You're making some people laugh. I said earlier that the question of the existence of god cannot be asked. It's such a hard question.

There are two aspects to your question. First, as I was saying earlier, god does not exist as some thing or some person. So far so good? Thus even if I say that god is nowhere, he is at the same time everywhere. If I say, as Christians do, that "god is Love," then love is at the same time nowhere and everywhere. You no doubt love certain people; you understand quite well that love is not a thing that can be located somewhere. Sure, you can send a card with a heart on it, but this is just a sign of love, not love itself. And so, in this sense, god does not exist.

And when you ask why or how god exists, then you have already begun to think of a person, a very powerful person who created the world—and this is something I haven't spoken about at all yet. Isn't that what you are thinking of? Now if one imagines god as someone who created the world, and if one understands creating the world to mean making it, then it's a little like imagining god to be like the person who made, well, this bottle. In fact this is a good example. Who made this bottle? A machine, a set of machines, no doubt, along with people in a factory. Probably few people and many machines. If I imagine that god created the world in this way, then this means that god is an enormous machine, with a very small brain somewhere, perhaps, but especially a very powerful machine able to make this huge thing in which we find ourselves. But that's going to pose all kinds of problems. Because we would then immediately have to ask who made the machine. It's for that reason that in the three monotheisms the question of creation is one of the most fascinating, the question of creation out of nothing. We usually use a Latin expression for this, creation *ex nihilo*, which means creation from nothing. That does not mean that god is a huge machine that makes a world with nothing as material. It means precisely that there is nothing there behind it all. It means: the world is there. When the world is there, there is thus either god, or the question of god, or what I tried to speak of earlier, the possibility of religion. But in everything I've said to you, it was never a question of the creation of the world.

What is interesting is that in other religions, in polytheistic religions, there is no creation from nothing; there is always something there. It might be called chaos, primary matter, or, for example, the great originary cow whose flowing milk makes the world. The cow and her milk, that's the first state of the world. This representation of god as maker of the world, of god as machine that fashions the world, was no doubt necessary, inevitable, so long as we did not have the knowledge of the world that we have today. That is why god was not. Because if he had been, if he had begun to exist, what would there have been before him?

Q: You were talking about the name of the Jewish god. How can people know how he is called when no one can tell them his name?

J-LN: That brings us right into the thick of religion. In the religious narrative of the Bible, god said his name to Moses. He told him, all the while telling him that one must not pronounce his name. That means that god alone reveals himself, that he is the only one able to reveal himself, to be able to say a name that at the same time is unspeakable.

Q: From where do we get the idea of believing in god? Because if god in the beginning created the world from nothing, who created him?

J-LN: I was trying to address that just a moment ago, but we would really have to have another talk just on creation.

Believing in god is something that is a part of all civilizations, all human societies, except our own modern or contemporary society, which no longer believes at all in god, or at least not in the same way. There are, of course, exceptions, people who are completely within a particular religion, who take up all its terms, who speak, for example, of the world being created by god. But today even someone who represents things to him or herself in this way understands, or at least should understand, that creation, or what is called creation, has absolutely nothing in common with the making of some thing. Do you understand that? It's not as if creation were just a bigger and more powerful making. If it were, it would mean that we were imagining god as a someone with great means at his disposal. The creation of the world is a way of saying that the world is there. There is nothing to look for before, because there is no before. There is nothing to look for outside, because there is no outside. Yet there is still the inside to be asked about. What is happening inside? What is happening is precisely that it opens, that it opens up, that it opens infinitely to something other than the things of the world.

This is very difficult, I grant you. But that is what a creator god means in the end. This creator is not something that can take the place of what physicists have analyzed as the first moments of the world. You've probably heard people speak of the big bang, or of what some physicists even call the first void of the world, which is never completely a void. None of this prevents there being something given at the beginning of the world. If it is given, you can always say to me that it is given by someone. It is indeed given. But the giving of this donation, of this particular gift, has nothing to do with an operation that would have taken place at an earlier time by another being from another world, because then all we are doing is pushing things back in an infinite regress.

Nothing: what is that exactly if it is nothing? I wish I had with me here an enormous book I received a couple of months ago from a German colleague in philosophy, a huge, five-hundred-page book called *Nothing, Nichts* in German. Your question is really right on. Let me try to say this. Nothing is the something of that which is no thing. Hence it is not something. And yet it's not nothing. It's the fact that there is something. For example, I can say to you that that glass there is something. If I take the glass away, there is no longer anything. For the glass to be there, there also needs to be nothing, otherwise I cannot place the glass there. If there is a bottle there, I cannot put the glass in the same place. If there had been something in the place of the world, the world could not have been placed there. Hence there is, precisely, the nothing. And the world comes in this nothing.

There is a very beautiful story in religion, in what is called a mystical form of the Jewish religion known as Kabbalah. It says that god created the world not at all by making something but by withdrawing, by breathing himself in, by emptying himself. By hollowing himself out, god opens the void in which the world can take its place. This is called the *tsim-tsum* in the Kabbalah.

I cannot even really say that the world comes out of nothing, that the world is in nothing. Nothing is everywhere. It's the fact that you can be here, that I am here, that the glass is here, that the world is here, and so on. Nothing is the fact that there is something in general, all of us. This fact, the fact that there is the world, has no rhyme or reason. But what's the point, one might then ask? God is perhaps always a way of answering: there is no point, no rhyme or reason, and that's why it is good. It is open, it is available. Available for any number of things, but at the same time for nothing.

Sometimes what we do best is nothing, doing nothing, letting things be. Now I am not telling you to do nothing. I'm not saying that the best thing to do in school is to do nothing—god forbid! Nor am I saying that when there are elections the best thing to do is to do nothing. But, more deeply, when one really thinks about one's life, about what one does . . .

A little while ago, when I spoke to you about joy or love, even about justice in the sense I tried to describe, what is all that about? It is really nothing. What do people who love each other do? Nothing, nothing but love each other. That doesn't mean that we must do nothing.

Q: Will we ever be sure one day that god exists or doesn't exist?

J-LN: No, never, because that is not the question. I can see that this is a very difficult question because it keeps on coming back.

If god exists in the way religions say, then this would be precisely the only existence of which we cannot be sure, about which it is not at all a question of being sure, not at all a question of knowing. It is simply a matter of being faithful. Let me return one more time to the example of love, or justice, or mercy. To be just, or to be not exactly in love but loving, to be in friendship. When we have friends, we are often operating in the realm of knowledge. We say: "I know that this friend has done this or that, and so I don't like him any more, he is no longer my friend." This is normal, and I'm not saying that there are not sometimes reasons for saying this. But nevertheless one also sometimes says: "If you are my friend, you are going to get over this, you are going to forgive me for this, you are going to understand this." In such cases it is not at all a question of proving the existence of something or other.

That is why, from this point of view, it can truly be said, and we would be in agreement with many people, with the greatest thinkers in all the great religions, that to claim that god exists or that he does not exist really comes down to the same thing. When one says that he does not exist, one is saying that he does not exist like someone or something that would be comparable to everything else that exists, but simply in a greater, more powerful and higher way. And when one says that he exists, one is saying more or less the same thing; one is saying that he exists differently from everything else that exists. One is saying that his presence, his existence, is a reality with which we have a relation that has nothing to do with any of the other relations we have with things in the world.

Q: Why are there people in some religions who believe in many gods?

J-LN: I went by this pretty quickly, so you're right to want to come back to it.

First, I would say that this shows that god can take on many different forms or faces. This does not mean that god is a being capable of metamorphosing himself, of transforming himself and taking on all kinds of guises or disguises. It means, rather, that one can relate to the principle of the divine, to what is absolutely different from the things of the world, through a plurality of gods. It is at this point that they become persons, or quasi-persons, each with a distinct name and each identified with a particular function. One calls on each god in a particular circumstance; for example, there is a god whom one calls on for births, another when there is a death, another so that the harvest is good, another so that a voyage is successful, and so on. These are gods from whom one asks something. In this asking there is always an appeal to what is completely other.

There is, of course, a great difference between religions with many gods and religions with just a single god. Everything I have said has been from the perspective of monotheism, that is, of religions with a single god. But, on a deeper level, there is something in common. We should also speak here of a very important form of thought that I don't quite know how to address. I am speaking of Buddhism, which is not a religion with a relationship to gods or to the divine, but which can nonetheless be presented as a form of thought or of spirituality absolutely without god. But it would take too long to develop this in any detail.

Q: How was god able to open the void for the earth when he was already in the void?

J-LN: Precisely, he couldn't. He didn't do anything.

That's what I was talking about earlier with the *tsimtsum*. At that moment, god did not open the void to the earth; rather, god is the void that is opening up. This will always be a rather poor way of putting it. You could ask me how it is that the void is able to open up. If I myself want to open up . . . But one cannot treat this as if it were the action of some person. You say: "How was he able?" but one might just as well say that it is a question of a sort of nonability or powerlessness.

Q: And what about the underworld [*les enfers*], and everything that happens after one is dead?

J-LN: Yes, the underworld. You are right to ask about that.

It's interesting that you put this term in the plural, because *les enfers* is an expression from antiquity and, before that, from Greek, Roman, and Egyptian religions. It has to do with the idea of justice, an idea of justice translated into human terms, that is, the idea of a justice that rewards and punishes. And so it's the idea that god, as judge, says: "You've done wrong, you are condemned to this punishment." Or else the opposite: "You have done nothing wrong and you are not condemned." It is a way of imagining or representing things.

It is in fact rather remarkable just how large a role this representation has played in certain religions, and especially in certain forms of the Christian religion, even though it plays a much less important role in contemporary Christian religion. But while this representation of hell and of the devil has much less currency today, it still has meaning. It's just that it does not have to do with saying, "After death you will be punished or rewarded for what you have done in life," but rather, "Are you able during your lifetime to be faithful to what I tried to explain earlier, that is, are you able to remain faithful to something that infinitely exceeds you?" This is hard. And it's just as hard for me as it is for you and for everyone else. Hell means that if you are unable to do this, you are condemned. It means that you condemn yourself. You condemn yourself not to burning in hell among a bunch of demons that torture you but, rather, you condemn yourself to shriveling up and withering away as you are, in your life, right now.

Q: When you believe in one religion, why can't you believe in another religion at the same time?

J-LN: This is complicated. In America there are Jews who call themselves "Jews for Jesus." In America it's sometimes a little like those restaurants that serve Cambodian-Basque cuisine. If you want to be strict about things, this is absolutely impossible.

I don't know exactly how this works for these "Jews for Jesus." It's certainly respectable, but it's contradictory, because the Jewish religion says that it awaits the Messiah, who will be sent by god, and Christianity says that the Messiah has already come, and that he is Jesus. Now, I might very well say, if we had the time, that the fact that the Messiah has come does not mean that he has truly come.

Within a particular religion, there is a precise way of figuring or representing god, what he is, what he does, and so on. So, normally, one cannot mix everything up. Yet there is something common to all religions, as I tried to bring out earlier. So I can understand why people would want to take a little of this and a little of that, why they would like one aspect of one religion and another aspect of another religion. At that point there is no contradiction. It means that one is not of any particular religion.

In any case, we would have to distinguish between the fact of being of a particular religion and belonging to a particular religious community. If you belong to a religious community, if you are Jewish, for example, if you are a little Jewish boy, you must be circumcised. If you are a little Christian boy, this isn't an issue, though you do have to be baptized. The two things are not mutually exclusive. So it's possible to do all kinds of different things. If you are a little Muslim child, you must pray five times a day. It is not the same prayer that it would be for a Jewish or Christian child; you are not going to call on god in the same way. So if you want to belong to all three religions at the same time, it's going to be a little complicated.

There are some people who do this very well. I'm thinking, for example, of the Japanese. There are many Japanese who are at once Buddhist and Shintoist. I won't even mention those who are also Christian, because they are really Christian only for certain ceremonies.

There is no contradiction in being both Buddhist and Shintoist. For the Shintoists, there are millions of gods who are present everywhere, in everyday life, presences of an order different from any other presence, but presences nonetheless, whereas, for the Buddhists, there is no presence at all. And these two things are not contradictory; each can very easily be related to the other.

Within monotheism this going between religions can get rather tricky. There is, for example, the case of a very great Muslim mystic named al-Hallâj, who was condemned by the Islamic authorities of his time, that is, long long ago, because he had practically become Christian from within the Islamic religion. There are texts of al-Hallâj that address Christ, all the while remaining within Islam.

While there are very clear differences in the way things are represented in the three great monotheisms, and even some very big differences between the three major forms of Christianity—Catholicism, Protestantism, and Orthodoxy—there is at the same time something that runs through all these monotheisms from the very beginning of Western civilization, and that is precisely the notion that god is the one who is not there, who is not someone, who is somewhere else, always somewhere else. In this regard, there is truly a great proximity between the Jewish god, the Christian god, and the god of Islam. It's even because of this that between the three the worst sometimes happens. At the same time, these three religions are incredibly close to one another.

Justice

You are not being presented with a text here, but rather with the transcription of a spontaneous talk, with all of its accidents and approximations. This transcription has been made with a great deal of care and intelligence, but the written form inevitably loses the better part of its movement and intonation. This loss extends to the point of distorting the meaning of the talk a little. Nonetheless, I have insisted on keeping this transcription without touch-ups other than in some minor details: I wanted to avoid transforming it into a piece of writing of whatever kind. It is necessary to retain within the trace of the event its character of trace, along with—since this is the theme—all the injustice this might bring. But it is also to do justice, albeit negatively [*en creux*], to the living word addressed to others, to what, finally, all writing must secretly refer.

I did, however, decide that it was necessary to introduce a number of headings in order to punctuate, for the eyes and for thinking, a text in which a continuous flow would risk offering no bearings.

Finally, I would like to express a regret here: I did not talk about the death penalty, although in my response to the second question it would have been natural to address it. I hesitated, thinking that the question would perhaps come from the audience, which would have been preferable. But then the moment passed. That the question did not come up shows that, for this audience, it was not immediately present.

The Idea of the Just

*P*erhaps you don't quite know what is just and what isn't (and from now on, when I say "you" this afternoon, I will be addressing the children and not the adults present). You probably can't come up with an idea of it on the spot like this, but nonetheless you certainly know what it is to experience an injustice, to feel that "it's not fair" or even that "that's a real injustice," as the cartoon character Calimero always used to say. Perhaps he is not so well known anymore: he's a little bird with a piece of eggshell on his head. So you do all know something about the subject we call the just and the unjust. A little while ago, a boy who is somewhere in the room, after learning that I was going to talk about the just and the unjust, expressly asked me "*Just* what are you going to talk about? [*De quoi* *tu vas parler,* au juste?]" This remark proves that he has an idea of what this represents.

For that matter, we could begin with this remark: "Just what are you going to talk about?" The boy who asked me this question—let's call him Simon—was well aware that he was making a play on words, even if he perhaps didn't yet know how to explain its subtleties. In posing this question to me, he hoped to find out what precisely, or exactly, we were going to talk about. That's not the same thing as saying "it isn't just," which has nothing to do with precision or exactitude. This difference between the "just," as moral and as opposed to the unjust, and the "just" of exactitude could be the foundation for all of our thoughts during this dialogue; we might even come back to it at the end.

It's easy to see that the "just" of exactitude does not mean the same thing as the "just" that is the opposite of the "unjust." For instance, one could say, "The contents of this bottle fills just two glasses." If it doesn't end up being the case, say, if the contents of the bottle fills only one and a half glasses, one wouldn't say that it was unjust. As with many of our words, our ideas, our *notions*, to use a more learned term, or an even more learned term that philosophers use, our *concepts*, we have an understanding of the word *just* that could be called intuitive or spontaneous. We know well enough what it's about, but we still have to open up the idea or the concept. Perhaps by opening it up, we'll come to realize that the word we thought we understood opens onto difficult problems and questions that we hadn't suspected before. That's what we are going to try to see together.

Let's go back to what I called the "moral" sense of the word *just*, that is, to what is just in opposition to what is unjust. I think that many of you would agree that what is just is what accords with justice. For the original title of the dialogue, we chose "the just, the unjust," the just being the quality of what is just and, consequently, the quality of what belongs to justice, and what is unjust being what is contrary to justice. A difficulty immediately arises, though, only a minor difficulty of language but one that obviously opens onto other problems. When I talk about "justice," many of you probably think about what happens in the courthouse [*au palais de justice*]. The courthouse, as you know, is the place where hearings are held, where judges sit, and where trials take place. People can be accused, defended by lawyers, and then judged, and what we call a trial results either in a conviction or in what is called an acquittal of the defendant. According to its everyday usage, the word *justice* makes us think, first of all, of the justice that forms a part of our large state institutions. There is a ministry and a minister of justice. But in the courthouse and in a hearing, the law is applied through being interpreted by judges, by lawyers, by the defendants themselves, or by those making the accusations. This justice, justice as institution, is not the quality of what is just. It is the institution that applies the law.

Is the law always just? All of you are prepared to say no, though perhaps you have no example to give as to why. We are spontaneously mistrustful of the law. I think everyone has a fairly strong sense that, if the idea of justice or of what is just gets confused with the law, then something's gone wrong. In a few months, it will be illegal in France to smoke in all public places, but for now, it's not yet the case. So which is the more just in this situation? If one can even say such a thing, which is the true "just"? I belong to the generation that saw the beginning of seatbelts, while you, well, you get into a car and automatically put on your seatbelts. It is a reflex for you now, but I was in my late twenties when the requirement to wear a seatbelt was first introduced into law. There were people at that time who were very unhappy and who found this law unjust. They felt that forcing people to strap themselves to the seat of a car was a restriction of their freedom. I was in a car accident at around that time, and I wasn't wearing a seatbelt. If I had been wearing one, I would have been less badly injured. Today, everyone considers it just that the law requires us to wear seatbelts. One could give many examples of this type of situation, for there are a lot of them. Similarly, you've grown used to there being a wide variety of given names these days, a much greater variety than was the case twenty or thirty years ago. Thirty years ago, there was a law that prevented people from giving certain types of first names to French children, for example, names belonging to the traditions and language of the Breton culture. Some parents who had given their children Breton names had to appear before a tribunal. This might seem strange and old-fashioned these days, but it wasn't that long ago, even if it seems that way to you.

So you understand well enough that the law isn't necessarily just. But that doesn't mean that each of us can simply decide not to obey the law, just because we don't think it's fair. That is another question. In that case, it is a matter of knowing how the law is decided, through which discussions of citizens or their representatives, and so on. For our purposes, though, consider the following: if we know that the law on its own is not always just, that must be because we have an idea of the just in itself, of the true just, of justice as an idea or ideal and not only of justice as an institution. So we have an idea of justice beyond laws, perhaps even of a justice for which there can be no law, or a justice that cannot be enclosed in a law, one that exceeds law. All of us have had the feeling or the sense that there is the just and the unjust without their necessarily being related to the law. Many of you probably know how it feels, in class or at home, to receive a punishment that was not objectively warranted. Some of you have certainly been punished because a buddy of yours was fooling around and the teacher punished both of you, or perhaps even the whole class. The role of a teacher is not to be fair to each individual: it is to maintain order for everyone. No matter, you receive an undeserved punishment, and you exclaim, "That's not fair!" You know other forms of injustice as well: a friend shows up with a new video-game console that you don't have—it doesn't matter which one, it wouldn't be fair of me to do advertising—and your parents refuse to buy one for you. That's not fair. But why? It has nothing to do with the law. The reason could involve money, the fact that your friend's family has greater means at its disposal than yours does. It could also involve the principles of your parents, who prefer that you not spend three-quarters of your time playing video games. Incidentally, this decision about your upbringing could be extremely fair with respect to your work and your future.

But I'm not here to play the role of your parents. You know, then, you have a feeling or an idea that there are such things as the just and the unjust without being able to give a general meaning or principle for them. For example, is it just for everyone to have a "whatsit" console? Maybe you're prepared to answer "yes," but how many consoles of how many different types is it fair for everyone to have? It's very difficult to take such things into consideration. If you read magazines or watch television, you know that we live in a world in which we are made to believe that everyone should have every console, every computer, and every possible or conceivable video game. However, you also know that all this has gotten a little out of hand and that it cannot really be an issue of justice.

So we have an idea of the just and the unjust, but we don't know how to define precisely what they are. We have a sense that they must refer to something in excess of the law, to something other than the law, and perhaps that they refer to underlying principles that would allow us to say what is truly just. But what are those principles? If one leaves aside the law as it is written in the penal code and understood by lawyers, what does one encounter? One finds another law, called "the law of the strongest." This could perhaps account for why the friend has one console more than I do or why he has a console and I don't, since he is stronger in the sense that his family has more money, which is a kind of strength. Many of you perhaps think that the physically strongest is in the right and that it's fair for him to win if he overpowers his opponent. At that point, justice has become confused with the results of a fight. However, I'm sure that many others among you think that the law of the strongest is not a law at all, and that it can't be a law. It is otherwise known as "the law of the jungle," and precisely in the jungle, where only animals live, the strongest dominate the weakest. So, the expression "the law of the jungle" plays on a contradiction: in the jungle there are no laws but rather relations of strength.

The use of strength alone cannot be just: that too we know well. Even if we are often tempted to assume that "might makes right," we know that strength by itself cannot be just. It is nonetheless a model that is often used: the films of Schwarzenegger, for example, though he has been making fewer of them recently, since he's now governor of California and no longer has time to make movies, those of Van Damme or even video games like Street Fighter. All of these deploy a model of the upholder of the law, of he who is in a position to do justice because he is the strongest, because he is more muscular, because he has, like Schwarzenegger, two submachine guns and three bazookas, and because he has the power to destroy everything. So we say that he takes the law into his own hands. This model can be very seductive; one could easily be convinced that this is what is just. Stories of this kind always take place beyond the law: the law is powerless and the police can't do anything, but then Schwarzenegger appears, demolishes everything, and saves the day. Effectively he destroys everything, but actually, he's always acting in the name of a just cause in these films. There is, for example, some poor little girl who is threatened by terrible gangsters. Even in Schwarzenegger films, even according to the view that the strongest are capable of making their own laws, we still find the idea that there must be a just cause into whose service that strength is put.

So deep down, we do know what the word *just* means. We know, for example, that it is unfair to divide a cake into unequal parts. It would be unfair, yes, even if Schwarzenegger did it, even if he came and cut a big piece for one person and a very small one for you. You know this situation well, for it happens a lot at mealtime. You check to see if the person beside you has the same amount as you do. Yet you also understand that it can be entirely fair to give a very small piece of cake to someone or, indeed, not to give him or her any cake at all. If a child is diabetic, for instance, it is dangerous for him or her to eat too much cake. So what is just for that child and for his or her health is to give him or her as little sugar as possible. We also know that it's unfair to pay less for work done by a woman than for work done by a man, but this happens very often. It is unfair, but the law does not prevent it from happening. However, it is fair to be paid more for work that is more difficult or more dangerous than for work that is less so.

What do we find at the end of all these observations? We all know that it is just to give to each what he or she is owed. "To render to each his due" or "to give to everyone what he is owed" is a very old definition of justice. The formula or phrase has been around ever since antiquity, so it really is as old as our civilization. And, although people have been discussing it during all that time, it continues to occupy us today; in fact, maybe it's not possible to put an end to this discussion. That's what I'm going to show you now.

That Which Is Due to Each

In saying that it is just to give to each what he or she is due, we have a pretty good definition of the just. Yet I'm sure that you see where problems immediately arise. What is actually due to each? We'll come back to this, but first we need to talk about a preliminary difficulty that is perhaps less easy to see. To give to each what is due to him or her brings together two principles under the term *each*. First, there is a principle of equality: "each" person is considered exactly like all the others. Then there is a principle of difference proper to each person: what is due to Nicole is perhaps not what is due to Saïd, and what is due to Gaël is not necessarily what is due to Jonathan. Thus there are two principles at work here: equality and difference.

If you'll agree, I propose that we call these two principles "equality" and "singularity." Singularity is what is proper to each person insofar as he or she is a singular being, insofar as he or she is unique. Equality and singularity are inseparable in the idea of justice, and, at the same time, they can come into conflict with each other, though perhaps not into contradiction. This gives us insight into something very important: the just and the unjust are always decided in relation to others. In the just and the unjust, it is about others and about me, but it's always about me in relation to others. I must be given what is due to me just as others must be given their due. This means that there can never be justice for one person alone; such a thing doesn't even make sense. So justice exists solely in relation to the other. It is for that reason that the notion of making one's own justice is utterly meaningless. However it is certainly true that each of us in our singular person has the right to a recognition that is completely particular to us. It wouldn't be just, for example, to decide that everyone had to have red hair or that everyone had to wear her hair tied back. To the contrary, the particular nuances of hairstyle make up a part of what each person is in his or her singularity, even if it is only a tiny part.

But then—this is the second part of the definition—what is due to someone? We're not posing the question here of how to give or render to each person what he or she is due. But one can easily distinguish some elements of what is owed to everyone: everyone has the right to live, so that means that everyone is owed the means to live, to feed himself or to protect herself from the elements. Everyone has the right to be educated, so it's fair for each child to be able to go to school. I am well aware that some of you are probably thinking, "I'm not so sure that's fair." And yet, schooling for all children is an aspect of justice, since to have no education or culture is to be incapable of developing all of one's possibilities throughout one's life. Likewise, of course, everyone has the right to health and so to being cared for, and everyone also has a right to those things when a particular fate—one that could perhaps qualify as unjust—involves being born disabled. It is just that people in that situation have access to certain kinds of care, that they be given the use of wheelchairs, perhaps, that there be access for the disabled, and so on. So it is just for those provisions to be put into place by the law. For instance, these days the law requires that there be wheelchair access in transportation systems and in public places. This discussion about what is just and about what must be recognized by everyone as being just in a given society could go on for a very long time, for there are lots of things we recognize as being just, in matters of education, housing, health, salary, work conditions, and the conditions of life. If we had more time to pursue it, this discussion would also bring us around to the side of the law. The reason why the law is always changing and evolving is because we realize that there is such-and-such a demand for justice regarding something that, up to that time, we hadn't paid much attention to or that wasn't very visible. So this would bring us, once again, to the side of the law and to what will always be in need of change, reform, and modification. For instance, we now realize that smoking is very bad for your health and for the management of what is called public health, owing to the treatment of all those who suffer from cancer or pulmonary diseases caused by tobacco use. It is for this reason that the law must change. The law doesn't change every day, but there are always good reasons to consider transforming it or to consider creating new laws, so that society can become more just.

But straightaway it must added that we will never manage to state exhaustively what is really owed to each singular person. How could one sum up what is due to each of us insofar as each of us is a unique person, insofar as that person is Nicole or Saïd or Gaël or Brahim? In a certain way, we could say that the only thing that matters is that the person be recognized as someone singular. It's an infinite list: at what point could I ever be finished being just to Nicole or Saïd? At what point could I ever be finished recognizing him or her, not only as a buddy or as someone who interests me because he lent his console to me or helped me with my math but truly to recognize him or her? Just by asking such a question, we can see how the moral sense of the word *just* could not be further removed from the "just" of *au juste* in the sense of exactitude and adjustment. There is no adjustment possible with the first sense of justice. If you like, we might say that justice is necessarily without precision [*sans justesse*] or adjustment. I can, of course, buy clothes for Nicole or Saïd, but it would be better if I bought those clothes in sizes that fit them.

(*Addressed to a child in the first row*) Sure, you're laughing now, but if I bought you a pair of jeans in my size, you'd look pretty silly.

So clothing must be adjusted until the person has finished growing. But what is to be adjusted when you're interested in the decorative aspect of clothing? What is the most just, a blue, black, or gray pair of jeans? Obviously it's not possible to say. Of course there are lots of things that are more important than clothes. There are things that each of us wants, things that make each of us happy, things that each of us dreams about. But there are also some issues regarding which we are not necessarily very just with ourselves. I am thinking about the diabetic child whom I talked about earlier. All of us, or at least a lot of us, like sweets, but it is dangerous to eat sweets when one is diabetic. Likewise, you often don't want to do your homework, and yet you have to. But if you think about it for yourselves, you can always go even further. There is no way to conclude the list of what is truly due to each.

Love, Impossible Justice

At the limit, there's only one thing that is owed to each, and that is what we call love: not only the love we find in love stories, the kind of love that makes us snicker when a boy kisses a girl or when a boy kisses a boy or a girl kisses a girl, but love in its broadest sense. We know very well that to love someone means to consider him or her for who he or she is, and to be ready to do everything for this person, to give him or her everything because he or she is owed everything. This doesn't mean that you are prepared to give anything whatsoever to this person, including what is bad for him or her. Obviously, parents and caregivers are there to try to figure out what is just and good. That's why there are children's rights that are not the same as the rights of adults. Adults have the task of thinking about what is just, even if they can never know exactly what it's about. An adult who is just to children is not an adult who thinks he or she knows what is just: you're going to study math and Chinese, you're going to wear jeans of this color, and you're going to take up this career—for if one takes math and Chinese, one can do lots of things, and so on. No. An adult cannot know what is just precisely because it is not a question of knowing. However, he or she must still strive to think about what's best, and in a direction for which in the end only love can point the way.

As a consequence—and I am going to stop after this so that we have time for discussion—one could say that to be just, once everything is said and done, once the minimum of what is owed to everybody is recognized, is to understand that everyone has the right to be recognized. I won't use the word *love* again, since this word can cause us to mix up sentimental notions with other, more serious ones. We'll use another word instead: *recognition*. This recognition must be infinite. It is a recognition without limits, so it's fundamentally impossible to realize it in its entirety—it is impossible to adjust. So now we can say that to be just is not to claim to know what is just; to be just is to think that there is still more "just" to be found or understood. To be just is to think that justice has yet to be done, that it can always demand more and can always go further.

In the history of the Second World War, those who were called the Righteous Ones [*Les Justes*], according to a designation of the Jewish tradition from the Bible, were people who, not being Jewish, saved Jews, gave them shelter and protected them against the laws that were, at a certain moment, unfortunately, those of France and Nazi Germany. Why were those people called the Righteous Ones? Because, in spite of the law, in spite of their natural affinities, not being Jewish, not having the link of religion or community with Jews, they nonetheless said to themselves, "People cannot be persecuted because of their religion. It's not a good reason. Actually, it's the most unjust reason in the world." It is totally unjust to say, "You are being punished because you are Jewish, Eskimo, Arab, Malian, or whatever." This is, quite simply, what we call racism and, in this precise case, racism as anti-Semitism. So those who were called the Righteous Ones were quite simply those who knew nothing about the people they saved or tried to save, often at great risk to their own lives.

All those people knew was the following: these people have the right to an infinite recognition, without limit, including at the risk of my own life. I am not saying that this idea must be the sole line of thought on the subject of the just and the unjust. But I do think the idea that would have to dominate our thinking is that the just, this time in the sense of the quality or the idea of *being just*, is giving to each person that which you don't even know he or she is owed. All you know is that he or she is a person and that, as such, he or she has the right to an absolute respect. You must think this for yourselves. No one will ever be able to come up to you and say "This is what absolute justice is." If someone could say that, perhaps we wouldn't even have to bother being just or unjust. We would only have to apply, rather mindlessly, what would be a law.

—Montreuil, October 21, 2006

Questions and Answers

Q: Which is more just, the left or the right?

J-LN: That's a very good question. If I can make a bit of a caricature of things, I would say that the right and the left are distinguished from one another by two different visions of justice. For the right, justice is given by nature or by the natural order of things. The supposedly natural way things function is just. There are, for example, inequalities in nature: some are physically stronger and others have more money, even if it is a little difficult to attribute that to nature. According to such thinking, it is only natural that they should remain stronger or wealthier, and justice is done when these supposedly natural differences are respected. That is why the right is not favorably disposed to the state getting too big. The state shouldn't impose too many laws, shouldn't legislate too much, since individuals have to be able to manage on their own. As for those on the left, justice is not given in a natural way, and so it has to be made. And for that, we have to search for it.

That, I think, is how one could differentiate these two sides from the viewpoint of justice. To be sure, we could be more precise about the matter; in fact, we would have to be. To do that, we would need to distinguish between two rights and two lefts. One right wants the state to have a very strong presence so that it can implement what is believed to be a natural law: for example, the fact of being French, born of parents who were themselves born in France, who were themselves born of parents born in France, and so on. This scenario invokes a sort of natural law, and so natural justice would be realized when those born in this situation or, to use one of their expressions, "good French people," enjoyed a privileged treatment in comparison to others. The right that is called "liberal" is something different.[1]

Similarly, there is a second version of the left, one that is practically nonexistent today but that used to think it knew of what means the mechanisms of the state and public power ought to avail themselves to establish a new justice through authoritarian channels. These two extreme attitudes, on the right and on the left, both boil down to the idea that justice can be "shown." To put it very simply, either justice is in nature or it is in a political configuration yet to be established. This brings us back to the idea that justice cannot be "shown." But there is still a fundamental difference between these two: for the left, justice is still to be done. It is first necessary to figure out what it is.

Q: When I found out what this dialogue was called, I thought you'd use the word *equality* a lot more than you did. In fact you haven't used it much, so I'd like to know what you think of equality and justice.

J-LN: You're right, I've hardly used the word *equality*. I did use it at a fairly central place in the discussion, but it's true that in what followed, I talked mostly about the difference that exists within equality. Your question also intersects with the previous one regarding the difference between the right and the left. Equality is the first principle of justice. There is justice when, at the very least, there is equality, when all individuals are considered equal. We could say that the first principle of justice is equality and that the last principle of justice is also equality. That is what I wanted to show you. We are in a democratic country, which does not mean that equality is assured but it does mean that the principle of equality is recognized. It seemed to me important to show that, although it's easy enough to know what equality demands in terms of the basic conditions of life, schooling, or health, it is less easy to know what equality means in the context of people who are all different and singular. This is where things get difficult, but justice demands that we think about it. We have to keep in mind, though, that we cannot raise the question of the equality of people in their singularity until we have thought about the equality of people insofar as they all have a certain number of needs that have to be met in an equable way. Everyone must have housing, shelter, and enough to eat. Everyone has the right to education, work, health, and so on. After those needs are met, another demand begins that is not nonegalitarian but that must extend as far as the difference of each person, one by one. Historically, before justice appeared in the sense that we understand it today, there had always been what we might call "a justice of equality." What that means is that, if you did something wrong to someone, then they had the right to do the same thing to you. But this has to do with an equality of strength, not a legal or political equality [*l'égalité de droit*].

Q: I have a question. At the beginning of the world, you said that things worked according to the law of the strongest. So how did the ideas of equality, of justice, and of injustice come about?

J-LN: The beginning of the world is not exactly the same thing as the beginning of humanity. At the beginning of the world is the jungle, the great primordial soup out of which, we are almost sure about this, the strongest emerged. But the strongest are not necessarily the most resilient. Dinosaurs perhaps disappeared because they became too big, too strong, or perhaps because volcanic activity was more powerful than they were.

As concerns the beginning of humanity, though, of course we know nothing about it. It is not by going to see *The Quest for Fire*, even if it is a good film, that we will really become informed about the beginnings of humanity. On the contrary, we have to think that the beginnings of humanity coincide with the beginning of equality and that the sense of justice is there straightaway, indissociable from men, even if they're also in conflict with one another and making war, launching their flint bludgeons at one another or barring each other from hunting the gazelles on each other's territory. It still doesn't prevent the word *humanity* from meaning "recognizing others as equal to ourselves," even if other things are, of course, going to cloud the issue, since some people are going to be physically stronger, while others are going to have more prestige.

One thing clearly shows that the first men were as engaged as we are with the just and the unjust, and that is language. Ever since there have been human beings, there has been language. And could we not say that language really is the most just thing in the world? For language to arise, for us to be able to talk to each other, there has to be mutual recognition. Language signifies that we understand each other, and to understand each other, there has to be equality. That's what I find so exacting [*juste*] about your question. You basically asked how we ever came to speak of the just and of the unjust. That's a very interesting way of thinking about it. At the beginning of a book called *The Politics*, Aristotle, a Greek philosopher from the third century BCE, writes that man is a political animal. Here it's not a matter of politics in the sense of the difference between the right and the left. Rather, Aristotle is concerned with politics in the sense that man is an animal who by nature lives in society. Why does he live in society? Aristotle says that man lives in society because he possesses language with which to discuss the just and the unjust. So you've just figured out the first chapter of Aristotle's *Politics*. Now you can buy the book and read the rest.

Q: Within the realm of what is considered unjust, can there be exceptions that are actually just? For example, let's say I kill you. If I kill you because I don't like you, that's unjust, but if I kill you because you tried to kill me, then that's just.

J-LN: First off, you're mistaken if you don't like me! I'm only kidding . . . What is implied by your question is precisely the reason why I abandoned the word *love*, because it is dangerous and risky. But all the same, I think we could have used another word that plays an important role for youth these days, the word *respect*. Only, we have to pay attention to the way in which the word is used, for *respect* these days usually means "respect for the stronger." So someone might be respected because he or she is a bully. When you say "if I don't like you," one assumes, of course, that it's a question of personal preference, which is, after all, perfectly normal. At the very least, you can't be forced to like people. After all, that's what friendship means. Everyone has his or her friends, his or her closest buddies, which is completely normal, but it does show us how difficult it is to think and practice the recognition of the other person in terms of what I called "love" a little while ago.

But to come back to your question, if I try to kill you, do you have the right to kill me out of self-defense? This is an extremely delicate question. One has to know whether it's necessary to respond to force with force. Of course, to defend oneself against an aggression, it is just to use force, a degree of force that is as equal as possible to that of the aggressor. But even if you physically defend yourself against an aggression, that doesn't mean that you're now in a position to judge the one who was aggressive toward you. Justice demands that you defend yourself, and if you have absolutely no other means available to you but to kill the other, justice will involve your doing that. But if you do have other means at your disposal with which to avert the aggression altogether or at least to overpower the aggressor, justice demands that you use those means. In other words, justice extends further than simply doing the same thing in return. It asks why the aggressor did what he or she did. That is how the great passage to law is opened up, to the idea of law as the social functioning of a form of justice. For instance, that's how the passage was made in antiquity from a law of retaliation to a law that, first and foremost, proceeds by way of speech and by way of an assessment of what is really at stake, one that asks itself how it should understand the other person's behavior.

There has been a law in existence for a very long time, the law of the talion, "an eye for an eye, a tooth for a tooth." This law refers to the legal arrangements of ancient Judaism that are found in the Bible. In this law of the talion, we already find the idea of a law involving an equality: if the other person cuts off my hand, I have the right to cut off his or her hand. But what is often ignored is that this law of the talion was established in order to prevent a situation arising whereby if someone were to cut off my hand, I would then cut off both hands, both feet, and his or her head. It was already a form of regulation, of moderation.

So I can't formulate the question in exactly the same way as you did. One cannot say that, within the realm of injustice, just exceptions exist. If someone wants to harm you, this is in effect unjust. But there are two stages in responding justly: the first is the elementary response that aims at self-protection, and the second comes down to a consideration of the person, which is obviously very difficult, indeed, perhaps impossible in practice. From out of this law of "an eye for an eye," something very famous happens in the history of our European culture. Even if you aren't Christian, you'll still recognize this line from Christ in the gospels: "'it was said to you 'an eye for an eye, a tooth for a tooth,' but I tell you, if someone strikes you on the right cheek, turn to him the other also'" (Matthew 5:38–39). Obviously it's completely untenable, this story of turning the other cheek. We could ask ourselves what it means, but that would be the subject of another dialogue.

Q: Are there just wars?

J-LN: That's also a very good question, but a difficult one. It is complex because war is a phenomenon that does not concern individual people but rather states or institutions. One could say that all war is unjust because of the harm it brings to people who didn't do anything wrong. To simplify things, we'll say that those people are caught within the logic of the states waging war. In a certain sense, there are practically no wars between states anymore, since there are no longer states for which one recognizes the right to wage war, either to defend their own territory or to conquer that belonging to others.

In a certain way, even though we still use the word *war*, there are no longer wars today corresponding to that former relation between states. Also, even if it was considered just to wage war in the past, this always fell, at least partly, on people other than those who entered into the war, on civilians. And there are fewer and fewer distinctions between civilians and the military today.

So what in the past could constitute a principle of justice between states—the right to wage war against each other —has disappeared today. Almost all the wars currently taking place in the world are justified by the idea of justice: it's said that it is unjust for a particular country to be governed by a particular person or that it is an injustice for certain economic interests to be threatened by some or monopolized by others. For instance, certain states have gone to war in Iraq for supposedly democratic principles. They claim to defend justice, a justice higher than that of all states. In other places, it's the opposite: rebel groups or revolutionaries are fighting against an established power in the name of justice. The contemporary world is in a very peculiar situation: war is being waged all over the place in the name of justice. So there are neither just wars nor unjust wars anymore. For that matter, there is no longer war in the strict sense of the term. We are now in a situation in which a sort of confusion has been produced between an idea of general justice ("everyone has the right to") and an idea of generalized combat, a relation of forces. And in this sense I think one could say that there is no just war today.

This question is not so easily settled, though. I am struck that you would raise the issue, given how young you are. For older people like me, it is a question we've been asking ourselves regularly over the past twenty years or so. "But can it really be the case that there are no just wars?" This was a particularly pressing question, for example, during the war in Kosovo: Was this war just or unjust? This question can only be raised within analyses that are no longer conducted in terms of states. First, in the Kosovo war, it was precisely *not* a state that was being dealt with but the Serbian province of Kosovo. This thinking is distinct from the old logic of states and concerns a general morality or an ideal of a great democratic justice. We can first ask ourselves what conclusions are to be drawn from situations like the one in Kosovo. Second, and this question is more serious, we can also ask ourselves about this grand idea of just and universal democracy:

How easily can it be distinguished from the economic, strategic, and political interests of certain countries? What you said is very important, because today humanity has to ask itself how to develop an idea of justice that is obviously no longer the justice of states that possess the right to wage war against one another. So this is one of those moments when justice demands of us that we return to the law and that attempts be made to formulate laws, in this case, laws for humanity. There are several international tribunals that judge war crimes, since there are such things as laws of war, but these tribunals are not recognized by all countries. It is as if, in France, you were to say "no, I refuse to recognize the courts in Montreuil." It can't function like that.

Q: My question relates back to that of the young lady. Do the accepted definitions of *the just* and *the unjust* have the same significance in all languages, religions, and philosophies?

J-LN: You are asking too much of me, especially as concerns languages. When you speak of languages, religions, and philosophies, you are raising very different cases. In a religion, there is one justice that comes before all the others, and that is the act of rendering what is due to the god of the religion. If the idea of religion has a meaning, it is to give priority to the right [*la droit*] of a god considered as a person who is superior to humanity and to whom it is just to give his due. This can be done through prayers or adoration, through a particular way of life or a particular way of consecrating his life, and so on. According to this definition, a religion cannot be just, but that doesn't mean that a religion is incapable of recognizing what is called the "justice of men," nor does it mean that justice toward god must come in second place. The point is that justice toward god must never contradict the justice of men. If it does contradict the justice of men, even if this justice is not perfectly established and fixed, we'd have to say that this religion, or what in this case was called "religion," is not just.

Q: I am asking this question for Simon, who is sitting beside me. How can we recognize what is just and what is not just?

J-LN: We can't recognize it easily. But there are simple things that can be recognized as either fair or not fair [*justes ou injustes*]: it is not fair that your neighbor in the cafeteria has a helping that is twice the size of yours. It is also not fair that someone be naturally stronger than another. I am not really talking about handicaps here, but even that someone be sicker or have more sensitive lungs or ears than others. These examples are easy to recognize. But what is truly just for everyone at the same time as for each person individually? This, one cannot recognize, since it is not given in advance. It must be searched for, invented, and found, each time anew. More is always necessary: one can never tell oneself that things are sufficiently just as they are. One is never sufficiently just. To think in that way is already to begin to be just.

Q: I am thinking of the Nazis, and even today, of the extreme right in France, both of which privilege one population over another. How can people stand to know that they're acting in a truly unjust way and to do it nonetheless?

J-LN: The problem is that those who act in such a way do not know it. They think they are being just. It is important to broaden the issue and not to limit it to the case of the Nazis, which is the great danger of this terrible history. It is especially important not to push this episode aside by saying that it was just these really terrible people. No, every person or every group of people convinced that he or she knows what is just and unjust, convinced that he or she is doing justice, convinced that he or she does not have to make the effort to become more just—every person of this type is dangerous.

The beginning of justice, as we have seen, lies in knowing that one is never sufficiently just. This principle is the exact opposite of the one I described earlier. Once again, Schwarzenegger or some guy in a playground who hits someone in the face is convinced he is acting justly: either the other guy deserved it or, if he didn't deserve it, it is just because I'm stronger than he is. This question comes up again in terms of knowing if it is just to take revenge physically. Without going so far as to talk about racism, you all know about the enjoyment many of us can get out of making someone suffer who is simply weaker than we are. All of you have seen it often enough at school, right? The weakest cannot defend him- or herself and someone who is stronger gets a cruel pleasure out of pestering such a person or getting into a scrap with him or her. But if you say to a guy (for it usually is a guy) who does such a thing "what you're doing is unjust," he might respond "Just,

unjust . . . I don't give a damn." That is one possible response. In responding like that, he is thinking the just and
the unjust in terms of a law: "I don't give a damn—I don't
have to obey the law." But he can also respond by saying
"Unjust . . . how so? I'm the one who decides what justice
is!" He who claims to enforce his own justice therefore has
his own idea of justice, and I might add that this notion is
not completely false. It has to do with the idea that every
person *has* justice in him- or herself or, better still, that
every person *is* a site of justice on his or her own, a site
where justice must be done. Perhaps I did not insist on this
enough. When I said that justice is always done in relation
to others, I didn't mean to suggest that I have nothing to
contribute and that I must only submit. But, in the final
instance, it does not fall to me to know what is just. Justice
is effectively made in relation to others. I am another in
relation to you, just as you are another in relation to me.
To the extent that I am only me, I am limited in my possibilities for thinking, understanding, and appreciating what
is owed to the other, what is owed to you. I cannot, on my
own, decide what is just for you and for everyone.

(*The signal for the end of the dialogue is given and the
audience applauds.*)

Now, is it really just to applaud? The honor of this
applause shouldn't really be directed at me—I have only
talked to you about things that lots of people before me
have thought about and discussed for centuries.

Love

*W*e call them "Little Dialogues," and yet they are never little. The idea of *little dialogue* seems poorly chosen; they are, rather, *dialogues for little ones* [pour les petits]. But what does *little ones* mean?

In any case, this will have to be a *great dialogue* today because we are dealing with a great subject. Of course, all the subjects are great, but I must confess that I proposed this one to Gilberte myself, whereas she proposed or suggested all the others to me. After the last "Little Dialogue" I did on the just and the unjust, I told Gilberte that love still had to be discussed in these "Little Dialogues." She replied, "Go right ahead, then." At the time, I didn't realize how very difficult a subject it would be to talk about, whether for adults or for children. The subject is obviously very important. We have to talk about it because we all have something at stake in the word *love* and in the images that go with it.

Up to what point, though, is it obvious that we have to talk about it? In a certain way, we could say that it is necessary to talk about love and that, above all else, love must be expressed. Love is expressed and, in being expressed, it is always being created. All of love resides in the fact of saying "I love you" to someone. "I love you"—we all say it and we've all said it. Even the youngest children here know what it's like to be encouraged to say "I love you," "I love you mommy" more so than "I love you daddy," even though both phrases are a bit conventional or scripted. And then there is "I love you," even the youngest among you have perhaps said "I love you" to other people of your own age, to others who are neither chums nor buddies or friends.

In a certain sense "I love you" says it all; everything is contained in "I love you." When we say "I love you," we say everything. We all know that we are saying something different from declarations like "I'm happy to be with you," to see your cousins, for example, or old friends. We're happy, but we don't say "I love you" to them. No, when we say "I love you" we are saying something really very specific. The question then becomes: What are we saying? What does "I love you" mean?

I can tell you that nobody can give us the meaning of these words, nobody. I could show you thousands of pages and thousands of books arguing that nobody can say what these words mean, or that the sense of these words is always beyond what we can say about them, that their meaning resides in the sole fact of their being said. When I say "I love you" to someone, the sense of love is there, but not necessarily in a complete or immediate way. I could be mistaken, or deep down I might not really agree with what I'm saying. But when we're saying it sincerely, we know that we are expressing the most intimate thing that can be said.

Intimate is the Latin superlative of *interior*. A superlative is a form that says something to its greatest power, and the Latin *interior* means "more inside than." So *intimus* means "the innermost of." The intimate is what is innermost in me, what is deepest in me, and so what is also most secret in me, most reserved and most properly mine,[1] inasmuch as this can be mine without my knowing it myself and without my being able to explain it.

When I say "I love you," I am saying the most intimate thing, both for me and for the other person, because I am touching that person at his or her innermost. For this reason, the topic is very embarrassing and difficult to engage. Is it even a subject one can engage? That is not clear. I'm sure that some of you were embarrassed when you found out that this would be a dialogue about love. There are different kinds of embarrassment, though. Perhaps you asked yourselves, "But how can we talk about love?" So you might also be uneasy and curious to hear what I'll actually manage to say on the subject.

We have all had such complicated thoughts and feelings at the prospect of talking about love. Perhaps you're ready to laugh or make fun of the whole matter. Often when young people talk about love to each other, they laugh about it. When children see lovers kissing in public, they laugh and make fun of them. At other times, we might look upon lovers with nostalgia if we ourselves do not have lovers. We know that laughter can often be the expression of embarrassment. We laugh because we are feeling something important, something intimate. We laugh in order to defend ourselves from the attraction or the fascination that we are feeling.

Moreover, some of you, or rather, perhaps some of the girls present, thought we were going to talk about "true love," about that big event that comes at the end of fairytales and romance stories. Although such stories are much less widespread today than they used to be, you still know the formula: two people fall in love, get married, and then have lots of children. This is not quite the image of true love that we have today.

Love is everywhere, even in *Asterix*. And yet all comic-strip stories—except romantic ones—addressed to children avoid putting their characters into amorous situations. In *Asterix*, love is treated in a humorous way. Even in *Harry Potter*—how can one not talk about *Harry Potter* today?—love is present. However, as always, the hero must be a little removed from love. The love story plays out between Hermione and Ron, and other love stories circulate around the characters. Love is all around us, and it intrigues us. Love electrifies us, and for very good reasons, since it is so intimate and important.

As I was trying to figure out a way to talk about it, I thought of the rhyme "I love you a little, a lot, passionately, madly, not at all." This little rhyme has perhaps been forgotten today. Do you know it? (*Expressions of affirmation in the room.*) Yes, even so. You say the rhyme while plucking the petals of a daisy. You pluck them one by one, saying "I love you a little, a lot, passionately, madly, not at all," and you continue in that way, depending on the number of petals. Of course you can also say "he or she loves me a little, a lot," and so on. If it's an ox-eye daisy, there are many more petals, so people often cheat by plucking them in bunches. Obviously they do so in order to land on "passionately" or "madly."

As I was learning about this rhyme, I found out that this game is to be played all on its own. If we don't cheat, if we take the first petal and proceed according to the number of petals, the game is a way of consulting one's fortune. The idea of fortune is interesting in this context, for an element of chance is always involved when lovers meet. We necessarily find those with whom we fall in love by chance. Certain people do meet one another in an organized way; more and more, in fact, one hears about people meeting each other through dating services and the like. But at the end of the day, there will always be an element of chance involved.

It is not the chance of the meeting that is important but above all the fact that we cannot meet the other person by necessity pure and simple. No one can say "you have to meet someone like this or that" in order to fall in love. And this is very important.

Let's leave the issue of chance there and take up the sequence of this little rhyme. It is wonderfully constructed. You wouldn't think it, but the construction is very fine. It's all there.

"I love you a little, a lot": You already know this is not love. If someone asks you whether you love them and you respond "yes, I love you a lot," you've already disappointed them. This means that "I love you" is absolute. We must say "I love you," period. We cannot quantify it.

Likewise if I say "I love X more than Y," Anne more than Julie, this means that I don't love either of them. "I love you a little, a lot" means that I appreciate you as a person, but this can apply equally well to objects: I like tangerines but I prefer strawberries; I like ravioli but I far prefer French fries with ketchup. I can also say it of people—I really like Steve or I really like Leila—but you know that this still isn't love.

"I love you a little, a lot" means that I find you attractive or that I like you. It means that I'm happy that I know you and that I get to do things with you, but the emphasis is entirely on me. I am giving an estimate or an appraisal of you and it's in reference to that that I can say "a little, a lot" or even more, "really a lot." But when I say "I love you," I cannot give you a measurement, I cannot say if it is more or less. On the contrary, "I love you" is absolute, that is, "detached from everything" in Latin, detached from every measurement and every comparison. This tells us something important: true love begins beyond every possibility of setting up quantities or degrees or of making comparisons. True love begins on the order of the absolute.

When we can establish quantities or make comparisons, by contrast, we are entirely alone in the affair. When I say that I really love fries with ketchup and that I really love Leila, it is about me: I am stating my taste or my preference. At this point, Leila and fries with ketchup have become interchangeable. So, at moments like these, people are being treated a little like objects.

In love, we are two. From the moment we are two, everything changes. There is no more degree, no more preference. One person addresses the other, and if the other person replies with "I love you," then the two people have entered into a unique relation that cannot be compared with anything else. It doesn't make sense to say that John and Leila love each other more than Steve and Roberta do. If it does make sense, the people in one of the couples don't really love each other, or else they're just really good friends. There are many degrees of friendship or fondness, but none of them has anything to do with two beings who have chosen each other in an absolute way. With love, we are no longer in the realm of comparison or of "I like/enjoy him or her." Of course we do take pleasure in each other, but that has to do with something else again.

I'm going to have to side-step two issues here, because if I don't, they'll take up too much time. The first has to do with what it means to love oneself. Loving oneself is not the same as egotism.[2]

The second issue has to do with the love parents have for their children and children have for their parents. As long as we still have our parents, or even if they have died, we are in a relation of love with them. But you certainly sense that it's not the same thing as the other love we've been discussing, since we didn't choose our parents and sometimes we have the sense that loving them is an obligation, one that we don't always want. Sometimes we don't love our parents at all, and that can also be true of parents as well. So this love is different from true love, but it does still have to do with love.[3]

Now I come to the third moment in the rhyme, "passionately." Passionately—what is passion? Passion means that we submit. Something happens to us that is opposed to action. Love happens to us. We don't submit to it like we do to a punishment, to an accident, or to boredom. Submitting can also mean that we receive or welcome it with pleasure. But we do receive it. It comes from the other person, from elsewhere.

We receive love even when we give it. That's what is important. When we love, we are giving love to another person, but we are giving something that we have received from elsewhere, from the other person, perhaps, beyond the relation to oneself and beyond the other's self-relation. This comes from nowhere and everywhere and allows us to address another person by being captivated or taken by him or her. We are captivated by this person because of his or her absolute uniqueness and not because of personal qualities, not because he or she is funny, beautiful, intelligent, or clever, not to speak of "rich."

If I say "I love Louis because he has the very latest video-game console," then I don't love Louis. Even if I say "I love Océane because of her gorgeous blond hair," I don't love Océane. Of course, hair and other qualities proper to the person do count, but what I receive in love or what creates passion is what we call the uniqueness of the person. It's him or her, and that's all that matters. There is a word for this, *the beloved* [l'élu]. Perhaps you've heard the expression "the one my heart has chosen [*l'élu de ma coeur*]." For example, in France we elect [*élire*] ministers, regional counselors, the president of the Republic—I don't understand why I am hearing laughter. We elect the president of the Republic, and he can choose [*élire*] his lover, but the two uses of *élire* are obviously very different. The election of a minister or the president is done by a majority. But the *élu* in love involves a choice that is not made by a majority. Choice here means that a person is chosen, distinguished or set apart from all others.

Old expressions like "the one my heart has chosen" make a good deal of sense. This expression refers to whoever has been chosen by my heart and by my capacity to receive, to feel, and to allow a person to come to me as a person, for what he or she is and independently of everything he or she has.

This difference between what someone is and what someone has, between being and having, is extremely important here. We love a being: reflect for a couple of minutes on someone you love, and you already know that you love that this person exists and not what he or she has, whether physical qualities or much deeper ones. All those things count, but it is much more important that this person exists.

Let's take another word you know well, one that will probably make you laugh, *dearest* [chéri]. You often hear your parents saying "dearest" to each other. This word is so completely hackneyed and overused that people mostly say it because they've developed a habit of doing so. It happens a lot that people who call each other "dearest" no longer hold each other dear at all. This is a case of habit and of language. The word makes us laugh; it just seems so ridiculous. I am thinking of children who make fun of lovers, not their parents, who aren't lovers anymore, but twenty-year-old lovers on the park benches of the Luxembourg who get on your nerves a little, so you make fun of them. You laugh to each other about how they're calling each other "dearest" and about how ridiculous it sounds.

The verb *to hold dear* comes from the family of *dear* in the sense of "this watch is dear" or expensive [*chère*]. To hold dear or to cherish [*chérir*] means to give someone a price. You might be surprised to find out that the word *cherish* belongs to the same family as *charity*—they both come from the Latin word *carus*, "dear." Charity does not mean "dear" in the sense of giving money to poor people. For Christians, that meant giving someone an absolute price. Christians gave everyone an absolute price, but Christian love is another question altogether.

When I say "dearest," I am using the superlative, which is the strongest in a series and which you can hear when adults say, also a bit conventionally, "my dear." In polite language, we say "dear so-and-so." "Dear" means that I hold you in high esteem, that I give you a price.

But if we can abstract it from all of its wear and tear, "dearest [*chéri*]" means the one whom I cherish absolutely, the most, him or her to whom I give a unique and incomparable price, a price beyond all price. You will be even more surprised, as I was myself, to discover that the word *caress* comes from the same family. In very old French, this word was *charesse*.

The caress is the gesture we make toward those whom we cherish, those to whom we accord the greatest price. This indicates two things to us: first, that it is a matter of giving a price or according a unique value to someone, and second, that it is also a matter of making gestures that correspond to this value.

What gestures might correspond to such a value? No gesture on the order of having can correspond to this value. And rightly so. Of course, we can offer gifts, and it is understood that we give presents to those we love. In fact, it will be Valentine's Day soon, and the Internet and all the stores are giving us all kinds of ideas for gifts to offer those we love. But we know that gifts cannot correspond to any love, and that they can even mask an absence of love. The gift can be a translation of the cherishing. But it can also translate nothing at all, or it can simply translate the desire to show that I have made tremendous sacrifices to be able to offer such a necklace, a diamond or whatever.

The gesture of love is a caress, not necessarily a sensual caress but one in which I address the being of the other, address his or her presence. The caress is a touch that expresses a particular affection. We avoid touching people we don't know at all. In the subway, we touch each other as little as possible. Sometimes we're forced to, but this is only because it's so crowded. And besides, if we do touch someone, it can be taken for a come-on or for the body language of an approach.

The caress teaches us that what counts in love is the presence of the other, the touch of the other, and, in a certain sense, nothing (of the) other [*rien d'autre*]. What does this pure presence with nothing (of the) other mean? It means that the only thing that counts is that the being of the other be in me, inseparable from me. In love, the other person does not turn into me, though. He or she is not identical to me, but still we two are inseparable. We cannot live without each other, as they say, without for all that becoming one, by remaining precisely two.

There are risks involved in all this, great risks. We can be mistaken, and we can confuse the image of the other person that we have in us, the other person such as we see him or her, with the real person, who is necessarily differ-ent from the image. Every practice of love consists in a back and forth between the real person and the powerful image I have of him or her. None of this is simple, and it can easily backfire. You all know the song by Rita Mit-souko, "Stories of Love End badly—in General."

Love opens onto a very great risk, but this risk is the measure of the incredible value we place on another per-son. We make him or her this valuable because we need to do so, because we receive something in return. Love tells us that things are never quite right with us when we're alone. We're not made to be alone, just as we're also not made to be in large groups. This doesn't mean that everything is automatically fine when we're with another person. But when we are with him or her, we know that "something's going on," as they say. We are made to be in relation with another person, one with whom "some-thing's going on"—something that's never definable but that's a real *relation*, in the strong sense of the word. I'm not saying that we are all, or always, made to spend our entire lives with one and the same person. It's true, though, that love does say this "love ever after." We do promise to love each other forever, but then sometimes it's all over three days later. But that's part of the risk of this absolute commitment.

✦ ✦ ✦

Let's now move on to the last two parts of the rhyme, "madly, not at all." In fact, we've already entered into the issue of "madly." There is a sort of madness in the risk, the engagement, in the very act of cherishing, of giving to the other person and of receiving from the other person a value beyond all value. We depart from all that is reasonable in terms of relations between people: we are engaged with each other more than we could be in any other relation. We open up to each other, move toward each other, and expose ourselves to a great deal, so it is very difficult to know at what point the other person might be asking too much. Am I right to feel that he or she is asking too much of me, or is the problem with me not knowing how to go far enough? This is an extremely delicate issue, dangerous and difficult. Such a powerful and unique relation between two people is very difficult. Each of them is risking a lot because they must both break from their sense of self-satisfaction and from their self-containment, from what is called "narcissism."

My calm is endangered when I'm in love, for love doesn't make you calm. But when a bracing disquiet tips over into a tormented one, it can't go on any longer. At the extreme, it's even possible for two people to destroy each other. The dream of lovers in all great love stories is of dying together, like Romeo and Juliet. Very often, old couples who have lived together for their entire lives experience the desire to die together. It is very difficult for these old couples to imagine one of them surviving the other and continuing alone in life. The idea of dying together suggests that death may be the only way of completely being together, whereas, by contrast, there is nothing more alive than love.

But there is also a sort of madness when love asks too much. Love is thrilling, and it can make you want to do anything. But in the end it can also ask too much of the other person and of yourself. It is a kind of madness, but all the same, it is a madness that shows its real worth, a worth beyond measure. Love demands a total freedom and a total devotion from the other person. Let's face it: in a very real sense, the demand of love is a contradictory one.

In the game of the daisy, we always hope to land on "madly." "Passionately" is already not too bad. Right after "madly," though, you land on "not at all," because it can all come to a halt or fall flat for no reason, just as it began. But that doesn't mean you have to give it all up after the first minor disagreement. If you do that, it wasn't love. But if the disagreement is greater and goes on for a while, it could be that it is both necessary and proper to break things off. The "not at all" of the rhyme means that love, even the truest love, can always be lost. It is never guaranteed. If a love were guaranteed, it would not be love.

We do make vows, though, as in "I promise, I swear." It is always necessary to make vows in love. But as the great philosopher Jacques Derrida, who died a few years ago, said, we know that promises would not exist without the possibility of not keeping them.

The promise allows for the possibility of its not being kept. In other words, a promise is not a contract. There is no such thing as a contract of love, but there is a vow. In making a vow, I am committing myself, which means that I want to keep it but maybe I won't and that would not necessarily be a mistake. This raises another issue, the issue of "Whose fault is it?" if it doesn't work out . . . Perhaps there is never, or very rarely, only one person at fault, but only the essential fragility, the terrible fragility and difficulty of love.

Still, the big word in relation to love has got to be *fidelity*. Once again, this doesn't mean that if love comes to an end or if one person is unfaithful to the other, someone is necessarily at fault. But that doesn't change the fact that the word of love is *fidelity*, which comes from the same family of words as *confidence* [la confiance] and *engagement* [les fiançailles]. Just as fewer people get married these days than they used to, fewer still get engaged. The *fiancé* or the *fiancée* refers to the one who promises, who bestows his or her confidence or "fiance," his or her fidelity, which comes close to *faith* [foi]. In the past, to say that you were "committed to someone," you'd say that you had "given your faith to someone [*donner sa foi à quelqu'un*]." This isn't about being committed to doing this or that but, above all, about being committing to being with the other person and for the other person, to being in a unique relation with what the other person is and with the fact that he or she is.[4]

—Montreuil, February 2, 2008

Questions and Answers

Q[G]:[5] I read somewhere that loving is essentially the same as wanting to be loved and I wanted to know if that's true.

J-LN: It's both true and not true. Everything is so very difficult in what you're asking. Of course, to love is to want to be loved. It's a request. If I say "I love you" to someone, I am asking him or her to love me too. I want the love of the other person to choose me and to recognize me as unique. I can live my declaration of love in such a way that this request and this expectation get the upper hand. But regardless, whenever I say "I love you," I am also asking for that which I give. I also can't say that when I love, I am giving everything without expecting anything in return, either. No, we have to say that, in love, the gift and the request are indistinguishable from each other.

Q[G]: In one of your parenthetical remarks, you talked about loving yourself, and sometimes we say that you have to love yourself before you can love someone else.

J-LN: I wouldn't say that you have to start by loving yourself, but it certainly is important not to hate yourself.

We have to be clear on what loving oneself means. Many philosophical and spiritual discussions have revolved around the idea of self-love. One form of self-love is a withdrawal into oneself, as if one were giving oneself preference over others. This is called egotism and cannot really be called "love."

There is another form of self-love in which we relate to ourselves as if to another person. In love we are two, so we also have to be two in self-love. One must love in oneself the possibility of loving the other [*l'autrui*]. In this case, I am not giving myself preference and I am also not withdrawing into myself. But I don't have a negative relation to myself of hatred or self-forgetfulness, either: I have confidence in myself as one who is capable of loving another person.

Q[G]: Why is it so difficult to say "I love you" for the first time?

J-LN: Not only the first time, but you're right, it is a little more difficult the first time. Saying "I love you" is difficult because we know how enormous this declaration is. It says it all, it even says too much. We're afraid the other person will reply "Not me." What are we waiting for when we say "I love you"?

"I love you too"

J-LN: Of course! A thinker named Roland Barthes wrote *A Lover's Discourse: Fragments,* in which there is a long note on possible responses to "I love you," from "Not me" to "Me too." Of course, we are waiting for the other person to say "Me too," because the only sense of "I love you" is that the other person love me too.[6] It is what I am asking for in giving my love. We know that we are declaring too much and that we run the risk of hearing "Not me." So it's normal to be afraid. The more afraid we are, the more we put off saying it and the more we enter into the truth of how a lover feels. But obviously, it's important not to wait too long, either.

Q[G]: Can we really speak of love when it is not reciprocated?

J-LN: Paradoxically, yes. I really can love someone who is unresponsive to my love. It is possible for me to love this person truly, for me to have discerned or touched something in them which they themselves ignore, something to which they cannot or do not want to give access. My love is not false, because it really is directed toward the other person. The response of the other person might not be uttered or expressed, but it nonetheless reveals a truth about them. This is a difficult point, and it would take a long time to analyze in detail. One might say that when we declare our love and the other person isn't expecting it, this declaration of love will reveal to the other person the possibility that he or she is capable of loving and being loved. Love isn't something I know myself to have at my disposal, ready to go. No, love must be revealed to me. I declare my love because the other person reveals my love to me. Even if nothing has been declared to me, something about the other person has come to touch me, silently and without his or her knowing it. At that moment I say "I love you," and I touch the very place in him or her from which my love has come to me. The other person might not know and might not respond. It often happens that the other person is taken aback or surprised and cannot come up with a response. For the other person can only answer "Me too" if he or she was already prepared to say "I love you." I can just as easily throw the other person into a tizzy by saying "I love you" as I can lead him or her to discover that, deep down, this was what he or she was waiting for.

Q[G]: Why does one have to say "I love you" for the other to know it?

J-LN: That's a very good question. Sometimes we do say it without exactly saying it: we show it, we express it. In a sense, "I love you" has both the advantage and the disadvantage of being said, of being expressed in words, but in words that say much more than they are capable of explaining. If someone says "I love you" to you and you ask for an explanation, the person will say "I'm not really sure. I do know that I find you very pretty and you're very nice. I'd really like to kiss you." If you replied "yes, but what else?" the other person will not be able to explain any further.

The behavior of someone in love can say a lot, however, whether we're aware of it or not. There is a certain way of being attentive to the other person, of taking care and of being thoughtful toward them, not to speak of giving gifts. It is often said that there is a look of love, and sometimes we make fun of it. For instance, we talk about the eyes of someone in love—we used to say "goo-goo eyed." When you're in love, you're a little naïve. You allow yourself to be amazed by things, and you don't pay much attention to people around you. You're ecstatic in a certain sense; you don't really see anything. But beyond the example of "goo-goo eyes," the look of a person in love really can say quite a lot about it.

Other than that, we sometimes also say "I love you" because we've had enough of the fact that the other person hasn't understood. It could also be that the other person has indeed understood, but that he or she is waiting for it to be said. As long as it is not said, in a certain sense, it is not there, or it is there as a feeling but not as a commitment or an engagement. As long as we haven't said "I love you," we haven't said anything. If you say "okay, so you're in love" to someone who's being extremely nice and attentive, he or she might reply "no, not at all" so as to avoid a commitment. "I love you" is already a vow, a formidable statement that we're afraid of. When we say "I love you," we're swearing to something whether we want to or not.

Q[B]: Why does love sometimes make us doubt the fidelity of the other?

J-LN: You're asking a question about jealousy. Love makes us doubt the fidelity of the other person because fidelity has nothing to rely on except avowed faithfulness, since that's all fidelity is. So we're necessarily nervous, at least at the start. We ask ourselves if the other person is truly responding to our expectations or if he or she really is committed in the same way as we are. We will never have any proof of it, or any guarantee. This anxiety is normal, it is constitutive of love. Love is fragile and apprehensive by nature. Jealousy is also a terrible and all-consuming feeling that can develop in a very dangerous way, since someone who is jealous can destroy a relationship if that jealousy ends up being unfounded. Why is it like that? Because in love we want the other to be completely for us. This feeling is exclusive. Being and having are on a continuum, which means that they can never be completely separated: I want to be with the other person and I also want to possess them. Possession is a part of love; lovers mutually possess each other. If something in me should push this desire to possess a little too far, I'll end up wanting to possess everything about them. I won't even want the other person to go out for five minutes. Some jealous people can go crazy. If the other person goes out to buy a loaf of bread, they ask, "Where were you? Who did you see?" So there is such a thing as a pathological state of jealousy. Later on, you'll be able to read an author like Proust who knew a lot about pathological jealousy. This illness is the development of something entirely natural about love. Without going as far as the great illnesses of jealousy, jealousy is nonetheless a danger to all of us, especially when we are young, since we are more insecure then, more afraid that the loved one will allow himself or herself to be seduced by others. We cannot always be sure that we're the most attractive one— and yet, what I was trying to say is that love goes beyond seduction and also goes beyond "pleasing."

Q[G]: Do you think that love can be eternal?

J-LN: First of all, as a result of being so conditioned by my job—because I am a philosopher—I would have to ask you to use the word *eternal* correctly, because it does not mean "sempiternal." Eternity is not what the scholastics of the Middle Ages called sempiternity. Sempiternity is what lasts forever. Eternal means "what is outside time." You all know the song by Dalida, "The Story of a Love Eternal

and Banal." But in everyday language we always speak
of eternal love, so I'll stop there with my pedantic little
remark.

Of course a love can be eternal. Our idea and our image
of love represent it as something eternal. A love can be
eternal, outside of time: it begins and then it no longer has
anything to do with duration.

A swearing of love contains the idea that love is everlasting, and this could not be otherwise; we cannot say "I
am going to love you for three months." That's what is
called a holiday love affair, the kind that fills magazines.
The trashy, *Gala*-type of magazine talks about such holiday love affairs and gives us advice about them. There
you'll find a morality, an ethics, and an aesthetics according
to which it's normal to go on holiday and go out with a
boy or a girl not even for three months but for three weeks
or even for one week, without any commitment whatsoever. This is not love but seduction. It belongs in the realm
of "I love you a little, a lot," even if it seems more suited
to the colors of "passionately." For a love to last forever, it
takes a lot of grace given by circumstances and a lot of
strength. It also takes something (but what?) that allows
for new beginnings or for continuations, because a love can
survive crises and infidelities.

Last year, the philosopher and sociologist André Gorz
died. Perhaps some adults here heard about the book he
published a little while before he died. He died with his
wife; they committed suicide together. Earlier, they had
decided to kill themselves when they became too sick or
too old, and they did it. His book is a letter to his wife in
which he tells the story of their life together. You can tell

that this love, which lasted an entire lifetime, was very strong, since toward the end of his life, when they're very old, he writes that he still loves her physically, that he loves her body and loves to caress her. Their common political engagement, through which they came to know each other, certainly played a large role. In addition to their love for each other, they shared a cause, an ideal, and a battle.

Q[B]: What's the story with imaginary loves?

J-LN: You mean when you imagine that you love someone?

Yes.

J-LN: Someone who exists, or not?

She could exist either in the imagination or in reality.

J-LN: But wait, these are two very different cases. For example, you imagine that you're in love with Lara Croft (*the boy makes a face*)—you don't like her, this Cinderella?

No, I'm not talking about fictional characters!

J-LN: So, you imagine that you're in love with someone you know?

Yes, that's it.

J-LN: This brings us back to the question "Can one love without being loved in return?" You enjoy imagining that you love so-and-so, but you don't want to say it or you can't say it. Or indeed, you know in advance that you won't get a positive answer in return. In your imagination, do you say "I love you" or not?

No.

J-LN: Okay. So, I might be tinkering around a little bit in your head or your body here, but one could say that you're creating an image of the other person and that you enjoy imagining their presence, but you'd never tell them so. This is very interesting and comes back to what I said a moment ago. In love, we bring about a division from the other. To the extent that we are carried toward the loved one by all sorts of qualities and particularities, we create an image of them that we carry around in us. This image, even if it has characteristics belonging to that person, is necessarily distinct from the real person, and a gap or conflict can arise, because the real person reveals himself or herself to be more than just the image I have of him or her or because I have idealized her too much. At the same time, we love a real person. This is all very delicate.

One solution to avoid such conflicts is to be content with the image, but I think that after a while you eventually will realize that it's only an image. But even when we do love someone real, it's important to recognize that we also love an image. So, things have to go in both directions, with the real person going toward the image and the image going back toward the real person. Enjoy what happens next in your imagination!

Q[G]: Do you have to want to love?

J-LN: No, because it's not really a question of will. I think it's very rare that someone isn't pulled by the desire to love, and very difficult too. If someone is not pulled in such a way at least once in their lives, this shows a real difficulty or a limit. But I really have to insist on what I said earlier, that at first love comes to us, that it is sent to us from elsewhere. The entire tradition represents love as a force, or as a god shooting arrows. So it's rare that love doesn't come, but, at the same time, it's not for us to want it. If we show no will or no conscious desire to love, that's just fine; we simply have to wait and it usually does come.

Q[G]: How can one know if one really loves the right person?

J-LN: That's exactly it—one can't know! Though we do have a number of factors with which to make a judgment about this, namely, the attributes of the person—from his or her appearance to his or her character. Then there is the fact that we don't meet just anybody. We are in a certain field of possible encounters, depending on how we live and on the extent of the openness given to us by our parents, which can either be quite broad or can be confined to a particular social milieu. So we don't lack grounds for choosing. There are actually plenty of givens, many of which we are not aware of, but what it is about the other person that attracts us, what makes us desire the other person—all that escapes us. The question as to why someone is more attracted to blondes or to people who are petite or thin is extremely subtle and, in point of fact, unanswerable. We all know that there is something in certain faces and in certain characteristics that creates a kind of echo in us. This is unanalyzable, down to the core. That's why we cannot say whether this person is the right one, since a lot of people have brown hair or have a particular type of intelligence, kindness, or charm. It is for that reason that I spoke of risk. But it is precisely because of this risk and this chance that it is also so beautiful: one is turned toward the unknown, toward what is so mysterious.

Yet there is also no right person somewhere out there, because that would be disheartening. If there were a dozen possible "good ones" that you first had to find and then choose between, love would become a society game.

There's another thing to consider: If a person corresponds to something of my dispositions, expectations, and desires and I declare my love to that person, and if that person also has a set of particulars which lead him or her to respond positively to me, the very declaration of love, the fact of loving, will transform this person. It will place them in relation to love itself, and this will change them. Love changes the person who is loved a great deal, just as much as it changes the person who loves.

We all know that love changes us. When someone's behavior strikes us as strange or peculiar, we say that he or she must be in love. This change is one of the many sides of love that we laugh about—we laugh and say "he (or she) is in love!"—because we are always circling around this core that is so mysterious and so powerful. Something very important is behind all this, and that is that love changes a person. A Scottish philosopher from the eighteenth century, David Hume, wrote something magnificent: he wrote that the beauty of a person is a consequence of the feeling they have of being desired. This idea is wonderful. It is an antidote to the beauty we get in magazines. It also upends the foolishness or the semi-foolishness about a toad finding beauty in a she-toad,[7] or about love being blind. It is neither of those things, for love makes people beautiful. And for that, we don't have to think about models in magazines. The beauty of a person is what inclines them to enter into relation and to present themselves. A person is inassimilable to any sort of model, canon, or image. That is why the image of an imaginary love should not distance itself too much from the real person.

Q[G]: When someone is in love with several people, can one say that he or she is truly in love?

J-LN: Your question is very tricky. I don't think so, so I would say no. I don't think you can be in love with several people. But it is possible that in the context of a very specific love relationship, another one can take place that has an entirely different quality or an entirely different tonality. This comes back to the question "Is this the right person?" This question is often asked, and it is difficult and painful to resolve, because it is true that the singular choice of one person does happen for a lot of people. For someone who is in love with several people, there might be no conflict if he or she is capable of appreciating this great difference in tonality. It is as if I said that I really love listening to Miles Davis but I also love listening to Stockhausen and

Mozart, without there being any conflict created. But there is no conflict in this case because Miles Davis, Stockhausen, and Mozart have no relation to each other. They are works rather than people. When there are people involved, each of them asks me to be entirely with him or her. The question is whether I can be entirely, but severally and at the same time. I'll let you think about that.

Q[G]: Why do some adults say that children are not capable of loving?

J-LN: I do think that children love and are necessarily within love. When a child is born, he has to be regarded for who he is, as the unique and irreplaceable being that he is. That is what it means to love a child, and parents are there to do that. A child has an absolute need to be loved, to be regarded as unique, in order to live. Not only do psychologists and psychoanalysts know this, but medical doctors do too. A child who is well taken care of but to whom not one sign of affection is shown, whom no one caresses and no one values, is at risk of developing very serious psychiatric disorders and certainly of becoming seriously ill. A child needs love. Whether the love of the parents is more or less successful is another problem. It's important for children to know how difficult it is for parents to love their children well. It is very complicated to address the unique person who this child is, because we must also help him or her to enter into various frameworks. Parents also project images onto their children: they'd be pleased if their children turned out in one way or another, and children will often do the opposite. That's completely normal, though, because children must affirm themselves.

So a child knows what love is, since in return for the love that regards him or her as utterly unique, that child also needs to address a mother and a father, or people who occupy a unique position in his or her life. So he or she is already in the love relationship, but the infant cannot be *involved* in love.

It is said that a child seven years of age has reached the age of reason. That's frightening, because children believe that they must have become reasonable by that age. But this age also represents something else. The child no longer needs to be cared for by the relation he or she has to the few adults who speak to his or her unique being. He or she becomes a little bit more autonomous. One could therefore say that the age of reason is the same as the age of love. Some of the questions that have been posed here show that, at this age, children can begin to experience love. At the same time, it is a stage. There are other stages too, ones that help us arrive at the age when we can well and truly get involved in love. But we have to keep in mind that, as Freud, the father of psychoanalysis, said, people never stop being born throughout their entire lives. With my sixty-seven years, I'm able to report that we do remain children for a very long time and that we are always reaching new stages at the threshold of which we can say to ourselves that we should truly be able to get involved.

q[G]: Is a narcissistic person capable of loving another person?

J-LN: Another narcissistic person . . .? I'm just kidding.

We'd have to define what we mean by narcissism. Narcissism can mean the experience of accepting oneself and of being at ease with oneself, of not being at war with oneself or not feeling despair with regard to oneself. This is a good type of narcissism.

The bad kind consists in doing nothing but revolving around oneself, or loving oneself in a way that is not about receiving love but about preferring oneself over others or about "I love you a lot." The narcissistic person loves himself or herself like an object, like a video-game console, an MP3 player, a Barbie doll, or a skateboard. Someone who is narcissistic in this sense is preoccupied by a quantity of possessions, and this prevents him or her from loving. But love is very strong. Often its first *coup*, or very first blow, can shatter narcissism or at least rupture it. When a relation of love is created, this type of narcissism comes undone.

(Gilberte Tsaï takes a final question from an adult.)

Q: I would like to make a couple of remarks. The first has to do with the word *caress*. I've noticed that, in different regions of the world, when someone asks someone else a question, they touch or caress the other person's arm as they do so. And my second remark involves the word *dear*. I have often used the expression "you're worth a lot to me [*tu comptes beaucoup pour moi*]," but I can't use it anymore because the word *worth* bothers me. It suggests a market value.

J-LN: The expression "you're worth a lot to me" does express love, but in a way that puts it in retreat. I hadn't thought of this phrase, but it's often used to express love by concealing it a little or to express it to a third person, as in "he's worth a lot to me." Some years ago, the Americans invented an expression to designate, mostly in official contexts, the person with whom one shares one's life without being married to him or her. So as not to use words like *lover* or *mistress*, which suggest infamy or infidelity, they invented the expression *significant other*, "the other who is important to me." This returns us to the expression *compter pour*: the person is important, he or she counts, has a price or a value. Let's gather these things together under the idea of value: there are use values and exchange values. Money, for example, has an exchange value, but it is also the zero degree of value because it is value as general equivalence. Everything has the same value, that of money: Whether something is worth five billion euros or one euro, the euro measures the relation. So there's a common measure.

Then there is a value that is entirely different from these, an absolute value, used in reference to what is valuable in itself without any possibility of comparison. People are of this order. The value of one person is not like that of any other. Earlier, I said that when a child is born, one has to relate to him or her as a singularity or as an absolute value. We don't question whether this kid is really acceptable . . . or not. We laugh at the very thought, but imagine that that is what the Greeks did in Athens at the time of Plato. The Greeks of that era practiced the selection of newborns at birth, as well as gender selection. They often eliminated girls because they didn't need many girls in the city. And if a child were born deformed or came at the wrong time, it would vanish. All of this involves a completely different world and a completely different culture, and we're not here to judge them. That's not the issue. The point is that, for us today, none of this makes any sense whatsoever.

Love is nothing but the relation to the absolute value of a person, the whole question and difficulty of which is that the absolute value of the person is also their absolute mystery. That is why love is so difficult and why it involves risks and dangers, just as it also involves beauty, strength, and passion.

Beauty

*G*ilberte didn't suggest "beauty" as the title for this talk; she decided the matter for me. She told me, "You have to talk to them about beauty." Then for a short while we tried to find another title, but we couldn't come up with one. So we agreed not to give it another title, for a very profound and serious reason: if we want to talk about beauty, we must talk about beauty *in itself*. We cannot use periphrases; that is, we cannot say something approaching beauty, as I did for my first talk, on god. In that dialogue, we didn't say "god" but "in heaven and on earth." This time I could not even have said "the beautiful and the ugly," since to speak of the ugly one has to know what the beautiful is.

So what is at stake here is beauty in itself and not something beautiful or "a beauty." It's common to call a beautiful man or woman "a beauty." When we say "there's a beauty," we are referring to one beauty in particular that perhaps has something to do with beauty, but we still haven't exactly talked about beauty. We also use "a beauty" in the expression "it is of a beauty [*c'est d'une beauté*]." For example, if I were in the Louvre and saw the *Mona Lisa*, I'd say that this painting is "of a beauty" that takes your breath away. It's a turn of phrase specific to the French language that when we say *c'est d'une beauté*, we mean that such a thing participates in beauty or that it has to do with beauty. But it's still not beauty.

A beauty is something beautiful that embodies, represents, or shows something of beauty. But it still doesn't show us what beauty is. To be able to say that a person is beautiful or that something is beautiful, we must have a certain idea of beauty itself or, if you will, of absolute beauty. This is exactly what I want to talk to you about: without knowing that we know it, we all know something about absolute beauty. In a word, we all know that absolute beauty is not a beauty existing who knows where, out of reach, which no one could attain, represent, or embody. Rather, it's something that shows itself as one particular beauty, and then as another, and another again. Absolute beauty manifests itself in many beautiful things and many beautiful people, although we could never say that this thing, this painting, this piece of music, or this person is beauty in itself. At the same time, we all know that we only speak of a thing of beauty because we know what beauty is. In listening to me, you are perhaps saying to yourself that this is not true and that we don't know at all what beauty is. You are perhaps thinking that, in any case, beauty is really very relative, that each person has his or her own definition of beauty—you might find something beautiful but another person doesn't, or indeed you find something beautiful on one day but not on the next—and that what is beautiful in China is not beautiful in Africa or in Europe.

But that's not true. We do know what beauty is. I want to show you that you know it, that we all know it. I am going to tell you straightaway why we know it, and then after that we'll try to fill in the details. You all know deep down that, if we speak of beauty, if we can speak of something like that, it clearly cannot be relative to the tastes of each person. If it were relative, we could not even speak of beauty. We would not even have the idea of beauty. I shall indicate this to you in a moment with words other than *beautiful*, with the word *pretty*, for example. We do not say "the pretty"; pretty in itself or absolute pretty does not exist. Pretty is relative; it depends on the person and on the moment. But the beautiful is another issue entirely, a more serious one. Beauty is extraordinarily serious. It's not just about what's agreeable or attractive. We all possess this vague and obscure knowledge: for a start, we know that the simple fact of being able to talk about beauty shows the knowledge of something that simply cannot be relative to personal tastes, moods, or moments. There is such a thing as beauty. But at the same time we know that absolute beauty is nowhere. It is no more present in the *Mona Lisa* than it is in the Sphinx of the pyramids in Cairo or in an African statue. It is no more present in Beethoven's *Ninth Symphony* than it is in Ravel's *Bolero*.

I think, then, that you also know what I am about to tell you. If beauty is not just about tastes or personal judgments, it is also not somewhere else, far off, beyond every real or concrete beauty that could be shown. For whom would it be visible? Angels, supposing there are any, and if there aren't, then no one would be able to see this beauty. If beauty exists, it has to be sensible or perceptible in one way or another. I think you sense that absolute beauty is in every beauty or in each of the things that we could call *beautiful*. Because it is *in* these things, something about them must go beyond their material presence. You know very well that when we say a beauty, a beautiful girl or a beautiful boy, we think that something radiates out from this person that goes beyond them. Something like a call or a sign happens in this person, one that goes beyond his or her attractive appearance. When we speak of beauty, we are speaking of something that goes beyond what is immediately given to us, by and thanks to this very thing.

Beauty is not subjective; it does not depend upon individual judgment. But it is also not objective: I cannot tell you what it is in the same way that I could tell you exactly what time it is. Of course, I can't guarantee you that it is the exact time because I don't have an atomic watch, but there are atomic watches that can tell the exact time. I cannot present you with exact beauty, but I can say that we all know how beauty addresses us, with a sign or a call through all those things we call beautiful. At the same time, those things we call beautiful are extremely varied and diverse, and we do not always use the term in the same way. For example, we can say, "It's a beautiful day today." What is more, we could devote an entire session to asking ourselves why we call this weather beautiful. We say it is beautiful because it is pleasant or because we like the heat, which is more comfortable than the cold and rain.

But rain can also be very beautiful. It is another side of beauty.

Standing at the sea, we can say it is beautiful either when it is calm or when it is rough. We say "beautiful" of many things in a very colloquial way, sometimes without even really thinking about it. For example, we say "the Arc de Triomphe is beautiful." Look, some of you laughed. I think a lot of tourists who come to visit Paris, and children too, do find the Arc de Triomphe beautiful. You also wouldn't say that the Arc de Triomphe is pretty; that would be a little bizarre. I am not going to get stuck on this example, for it would take too long to analyze why you don't really think of the Arc de Triomphe as beautiful. Perhaps it has force or power, but that's something different. The Eiffel Tower is beautiful. Aha! Now you're not laughing.

There is something common to all these examples. When we say that something is beautiful, whether it be the Eiffel Tower, a beautiful girl, a good-looking boy, or a beautiful horse, we are always saying that, at the very least, it pleases us. That's the first thing. What is it to please? To please is to attract. When something pleases me, I am attracted. The perception of something that we call beautiful gives birth to a desire in us.

I am going to play a first piece of music by Monteverdi for you now, *The Lament of Ariadne*. When you hear this music and this singer, it doesn't please you in the same way that your usual music does, whether you're into rap or rock, but you do feel something in the music that attracts you, that pulls you. Toward what are we being attracted?

Toward nothing, in a certain sense, if not toward the hearing of this voice and of what we experience as a kind of plaintive moaning. Ariadne has been abandoned. She is not just in pain; she's suffering an affliction. We are attracted by the very thing, the melody, the timbre of her voice, its purity, the delicacy of its modulations. We are attracted by what we are hearing, but at the same time, and through it, we are attracted toward nothing we could name or grasp. We could do a musicological or even a physiological analysis of this voice, but that would teach us nothing about how it makes something open up in us that is on the order of a desire that goes nowhere if not beyond or farther. Through this voice, something attracts us and calls us beyond the simple act of listening. But this "beyond" happens in the listening; because it is beautiful, this music resonates in me and I resonate with it.

You also know that it is not simply pleasant or agreeable. You know how to tell the difference between what is pleasant or what we like to listen to and what is more than pleasant. We are touching here on the essential point of what constitutes beauty. There is what is simply pleasant and then there is what pleases beyond its simply being pleasant. There is what is agreeable and what is more than agreeable, what can even be disagreeable or can go too far but can still concern beauty. There is that which is pretty, pleasant, stunning, graceful, captivating, successful, well-done, super, that which pleases us right away. The dividing line between the domains of the beautiful and the pretty is not at all clear, between a pleasure which opens up the desire for beauty and that which pleases in a simple and immediate way. We can perceive the same piece of music or the same image in a way that remains on the order of the pretty and then, at another moment, in a way that is opened onto beauty. I believe you all know that saying "that is super" is not the same as saying "that is beautiful." Most of the time, we don't confuse the two phrases. In the one case, we use a whole series of phrases in the first person, such as "I like" or "I adore," whereas in the other, we say "that is beautiful." You might want to tell me that we also say "that is stunning." But first and foremost, what is to be understood by this expression is "I am stunned." So, you have a sense that I cannot relate the beautiful to my own judgment. It is not about my pleasure or approval, so it is not about the agreeable.

The beautiful awakens in us an attraction, a desire that is stronger than simple pleasure, a desire that is not satisfied with the object. This desire goes further than that. I will now show you a painting by an Italian painter named Caravaggio, from the end of the Italian Renaissance. This painting represents Narcissus, the boy who one day sees his image in a pool of water. He finds that image so beautiful that he desires it, falls into the water after it, and then drowns. On the edge of the bank where he drowns, a flower grows that we call "narcissus."

This story is often interpreted as a terrible misfortune, since Narcissus was in love with himself. It is important not to be in love with oneself, not to fall into what psychoanalysis calls "narcissism." So Narcissus was punished for being in love with himself. I think that this interpretation is false, even if it does tell us something about the origins of myth. The story of Narcissus actually conveys something very different from what this interpretation suggests.

This boy doesn't ever see himself. He doesn't recognize himself, and so he doesn't know that he's looking at himself. He sees this face that he finds beautiful, this face of such beauty that he passionately desires it and will ultimately lose himself in it. He sees a stranger. So the myth of Narcissus is not about self-obsession, since, when I look at myself in the mirror, I know it's me, whereas that's not the case with Narcissus. At the moment when Narcissus sees himself in the water, his gaze is that of someone who is seeing beauty. This is not someone gazing at himself in a narcissistic fashion. It is the gaze that is opened onto beauty seeing itself, and, seeing itself, it also sees this relation to beauty and loses itself in that relation in order to reemerge in the form of a beautiful flower. The gaze is discovered to be capable of beauty and also to be capable of perceiving beauty right up to the point of losing itself in it.

In this painting, Caravaggio represents the scene on a distinctly vertical plane; the reflection sends everything back into a vertical and frontal dimension for we who are looking at it. So we are made to understand that our own gaze at the painting is of the same order as Narcissus' gaze at his own image. For Caravaggio, the image of Narcissus is fundamentally a representation of the art of painting in general. My gaze, which comes toward the horizontal plane of the painting, pivots onto the vertical plane and joins up with the gaze of Narcissus looking at himself. Every time we look at a painting or something on the order of art, we are in a relation to something that takes us beyond the simple gaze, beyond the simple fact of looking at an image, of understanding it and of finding it more or less agreeable. There can even be something in the image that is difficult to grasp. It is not simply pleasant; it asks that we become attached to it and that we understand it. And yet, the rendering of the colors and the lines of the picture here is not sufficiently well-done for us to enter into this image in as profound a way as would be necessary. Every time we are dealing with a beautiful image, we are dealing with an image in which beauty pulls us further than the image, into the depths of the image just as Narcissus is pulled into the depths of the water. We might say the following: when I say that what is beautiful in a beautiful image or a beautiful piece of music carries us further than the image or the music themselves and that this "further" is beauty, I am saying something that in philosophical terms is called "the universal." I am saying that there is a universality of the beautiful, that the beautiful is universal, and that it holds for everyone. You're now going to tell me that the Caravaggio painting we just looked at is not universal at all because it doesn't mean much to some of you or to Africans or to Chinese people who live in very different cultures where even the play of forms and colors are not the same, let alone the stories told.

But remember what I just said. Beauty is nowhere. When I say that it's universal, I don't mean that it is suspended somewhere in the sky, where it would be universal but invisible. This makes no sense because beauty must be visible. If there is a universality of the beautiful, this universality is not given. It is appealed to [appelée], offered, desired. It is held out to us. If it were simply given to us, at the very moment when beauty was given, there would no longer be beauty, because there would no longer be desire or the call [*appel*]. In the same way, if I were to tell you that the universal time is three-fifty-two, you would lose all interest in it. To want to know what time it is is more interesting.

Kant, the German philosopher from the end of the eighteenth century who tried to explain judgments about beauty, says that, unlike judgments about the agreeable, judgments about beauty have a universal aim. If I say "this is beautiful," I am claiming that my judgment can have a universal value even if I know that it can't have that value in any immediate way. I am aiming at universality. But if I say "I like this," I am admitting that this judgment concerns me alone. When I say "this is beautiful," I am suggesting to others, as to myself, that they relate to something that is not individual, subjective, or relative.

Let's look at another painting, *The Reading*, by Édouard Manet, a French painter from the end of the nineteenth century. It depicts a scene that is very different from that of *Narcissus*. A young man is reading to a young girl. This boy is reading to this girl, and something seems to be going on. Perhaps he is reading to her in order to impress her, but is it only about that? Why was this painting done? To place this profusion of whiteness before our eyes: the dress of the young girl, the white fabric that covers the seat and the curtains. What is going on in this painting? Something between the whiteness, the bright and transparent light— look at the sleeves hinting at the arms underneath—and the darkness. Something is going on between this brilliant transparent white and this darkness, the black of the boy's dress. Curiously, we see a black square on the page of the book, which is perhaps a shadow but which also seems to plunge the writing of the book itself into darkness. Something is going on here that is wholly in the relation between the light and the darkness, the brilliance of the visible and the darkness of the book. Perhaps this is a way of saying that the visible, the brilliant, the white, the transparent are on the side of woman, of seduction, of beauty. The painting does not really show us whether or not the man is beautiful. He is in the darkness, but he is also on the side of reading, of the readable. The visible is gesturing toward a sense that is more than that of the readable. Perhaps that is why the page is almost obstructed by a sort of black rectangle. In a painting like this one, from the very first viewing we understand that what matters is not the story being told. In a certain way it doesn't even really tell a story, or the bit of a story it does tell serves as a support for that other thing that we can neither recount nor write, for something that is given through the whiteness, the brilliance, the transparency, and, I would say, for a striving toward the light, to go into it, to let oneself be taken or carried away by it.

This going into the light or this getting carried into something that, through the form, goes beyond it and makes us go further—all this makes us look at the image more than once. In other words, it's not an image from a magazine. Those are made for page turning: you see Carla Bruni, and then you turn the page. You see Naomi Campbell, and then you turn the page, and so on. You also see beautiful photographs of landscapes or the earth as it is seen from a helicopter. These photographs are pleasant, but you still turn the page. When you see paintings or photographs taken with the intention of creating a work of art, you cannot turn the page. You have to stop at it, you have to return to it. The two paintings I just showed you, just like the piece of music I had you listen to, are works that millions of people have returned to. There they discover another accent, another variation on the same key. And in effect, it is always about the same desire, the same call, and the same striving toward beauty. When I say "toward beauty," perhaps you understand better now that this is not a call toward something that is elsewhere. The thing is there, and it is there for us to sink into, just as Narcissus does in the water, and in the whiteness and transparency of the dress in the Manet painting.

This applies to every image. Let's look at a prehistoric painting, that is, from the origins of what we call art. I don't remember which cave this stag comes from, but I simply wanted to point out to you very briefly that the role of these paintings has been the subject of much discussion. Why were they painted? Was it a magical practice to ensure a good hunt or a religious practice? Even the look of the drawing and the color shows that the person who painted it was already attentive to beauty. As soon as it is a question of the human, we find art and this call toward beauty. It is clear that, in this painting, perhaps even more important than the pleasure of representing the animal is the desire to touch beauty and to make it touch.

Here is another, completely different image, of an Amazonian statue. I don't know anything about this statue, but I saw it and decided to choose it for this talk because of how obvious it is that, even if this statue has many different sacred, totemic, or mythological functions, the work of forms can never be reduced to these functions. This work shows something other than its functions for a humanity of a completely different civilization than our own, one that has other shapes and other colors in its spirit. But once again, through all this, it is about a relation to beauty at the same time as it is about other things as well.

One last image, a painting by a French painter who died only a few months ago, Simon Hantaï. This canvas represents nothing. It was made using a technique that he invented. He folded the canvas and then knotted it at the folds. After that, he poured paint onto it and then unfolded it. In the unfolding, the areas where the paint was able to set appeared and those where it did not take were left white. We can't be relating to a story anymore, or to a magical or religious function. This painting shows exactly the opening of the canvas to the relations of the color and the white, to the folds, to the splatters, to something that is almost nothing. Hantaï loved to say that there was nothing to see, nothing to look for. This nothing is at the same time a pure opening or an unfolding of our gaze, thanks to the canvas that opens onto beauty.

Where a beautiful piece of art is concerned, we might say that what distinguishes it from what is pretty or pleasing is how the form of the work takes pleasure in itself. The pleasure is not so much for us but is in the thing itself. The thing does not please itself in the same way that it pleases us. It does not indulge itself; it has nothing to take or to savor. This pleasure that the form takes in itself is what can open us up to this dimension beyond all pleasure and beyond any instant gratification. That doesn't mean it offers no satisfaction, just that it doesn't stop at that point.

Beauty can never make do with simply being suitable for whatever, whether for one's own personal preferences or the preferences of an age or a society for particular styles or conventions. The forms in a Caravaggio painting or those in Monteverdi's music do suit a certain set of conventions, of styles or ways belonging to an era. In that sense, the painting of Hantaï would have been impossible in the age of Caravaggio, and the painting of Manet would have been impossible at the time of the prehistoric stag. Personal preferences or those of a society or fashion cannot, though, enter into the form of the work itself. Of course, where fashion is concerned, there can be appeals and references to beauty, but the way we dress is primarily dictated by the rules and codes that a society sets for itself. Addicts that you are to fashion labels, you nonetheless know that beauty is not what is at stake, even if you say that your brand X running shoes are beautiful. I am not in a position to speak ill of this preference, but we all know that something other than preference is at stake when we speak of beauty. Or if it is a preference, it is for something that is in us and that surpasses us. This thing is called "truth." In beauty, it is a question of truth. It is not a verifiable truth, but the truth as that toward which we are called, pulled, in a desire that goes well beyond us. Since the time of the ancient Greeks, one sentence has summarized the thought of at least two great authors of antiquity, Plato and Plotinus, although it is not found explicitly stated in either of these two writers' oeuvres: "Beauty is the radiance of the true." This means not only that the true shines, but that truth, more than being truth, radiates or shines.

We must also admit that there is always something unsettling in the beautiful. If beauty is not simply pleasing but pleases in the mode of a call more than of pleasure, this is also because it unsettles. Let's quickly go over these images again. Looking at each of them, I think you can make out the disquieting aspect of each quite easily; we cannot rest content with being before a pleasant image. There is nothing reassuring about these images. They destabilize and unsettle us: We ask ourselves what is to be found behind them or where that might take us. We know nothing about it, though, and so we certainly can't conclude that we've found beauty and so now we're satisfied.

I would like to finish by citing an important French poet from the beginning of the twentieth century, Arthur Rimbaud, who begins his most important text, *A Season in Hell,* with the following: "One night I took Beauty in my arms—and I thought her bitter—and I insulted her." Beauty as a received convention or as what is agreed upon by an entire era became unbearable to him. But forty pages later, after going through all the criticisms of this world of rigid conventions, Rimbaud ends by saying: "That's all past. These days I know how to greet Beauty." We only know how to greet beauty once we are freed from all that is conventional, whether that be a personal preference or those dictated by the customs of a society.

—Montreuil, January 10, 2009

Questions and Answers

q: I'd like to know whether beauty can be ephemeral.

j-ln: That's a beautiful question. I would say that at the material level, beauty can certainly be fleeting: imagine a landscape, or a rainbow about to vanish from the sky after a thunderstorm. But beauty is both fleeting and eternal at the same time. The painter who attempts to capture this moment doesn't want just to reproduce it but to capture whatever made him or her feel the call of beauty. This is what he or she puts on the canvas. Of course, the canvas isn't everlasting, since even if remains in existence for a very long time, it will eventually deteriorate. "Eternal" doesn't mean what lasts for a long time; it means what is outside time. I'd like to recount an anecdote for you from Jean-Luc Godard, the filmmaker. For cinema also has to do with beauty; it is not just about movies like *Star Wars* or *Harry Potter*. The anecdote might be made up—perhaps by Godard himself?—but it doesn't really matter, it's still well-done. At any rate, he's driving with his cameraman along a highway in Switzerland—he himself is Swiss—and he sees a remarkable sky, so they stop and start to film. The police arrive and tell them that they are not allowed to park on the emergency shoulder, at which point Godard says to them: "Yes I know. But there is an emergency; look at this sky." This is a lovely little story about the ephemeral and the eternal.

q: When we find something or someone beautiful, what do we look at first?

J-LN: This question is strange because it reverses the order of things. If we find someone or something beautiful, then we've already looked at them. But I don't think that means we've looked at anything in particular. It also doesn't mean that we've taken in the whole, but the whole does give off a quality that makes us feel as if there is more than meets the eye. I'll use the example of a person. If I find someone pretty, this means I've seen particular things that suit my taste. It could be the hair, for instance, or the dress. In everyday conversation, we sometimes have the sense that *pretty* and *beautiful* are words that mean different things. For instance, someone says that so-and-so is pretty, and another says she's not pretty but beautiful. We all know what it means to go from pretty to beautiful. A beautiful person is someone who's not necessarily very pretty but who does have something beyond their relation to a certain set of conventions. A supermodel is an example of this kind of relation to conventions. I cannot give an example of a supermodel whom I would call beautiful. It is not about the individual people: maybe they are beautiful outside their role as supermodels. Someone's beauty also includes his or her thinking and relationship to us. A beautiful person is not simply attractive: perhaps the more attractive someone is to us, the less likely it will be that he or she is able to show beauty. The more we experience what is beyond him or her and beyond us—which merits the name of truth— the more beautiful will he or she appear.

Q: Can we find beauty in everything?

J-LN: Yes. I sound as if I'm taking a firm stance here, but actually I'm not entirely sure. Let's take one of the least beautiful things in this room: this bottle of mineral water. It is not really beautiful. I can't find anything beautiful in this object, and we can't include the label in the order of beauty either, since it simply states things: the brand, for instance, or the contents' composition. Yet I could perform some sort of gesture that would put it in relation to beauty, like the gesture of an artist. I'm not an artist, but I could pretend to be. If I were arrested by the transparency of the plastic or by its shine, if I were to cut up a picture of this bottle and work it up, I could transform it into a photograph or into a painting. I could do an installation using bottles filled with colored water. I could draw beauty out of it; I could go beyond this object and pass into an order that's no longer of the object, in the same way that the paintings I showed you aren't objects. Of course, a painting is a canvas with paint on it, but what counts as a picture is not an object. What do we call it if it is neither an object nor a subject in the sense that a person is said to be a subject? I would say that it's . . .

Art?

J-LN: Yes, but what's art? Art is the human activity that deals only with beauty.

Q: When you say "beauty," you are talking about physical beauty, but can inner beauty also be called "beauty"?

J-LN: There is no such thing as inner beauty per se. Beauty necessarily has to be perceived. It can be visible or audible, or a combination of the two. I could put what I just said about a beautiful person into your terms. I have no reason to talk about the inner prettiness of a good-looking person. In fact, it doesn't even occur to me to think about his or her interior. Strangely enough, when I do think about the inside of a good-looking person, I automatically think about his or her anatomy—the skeleton and organs. This becomes quite awful, almost repulsive. If I were to talk about a beautiful person in this way, what I would mean is that his or her external appearance expresses something of the interior.

Were I to develop this thought further, I would broach something I didn't have time to talk about earlier, which is why Gilberte asked me to talk about beauty. She asked me because of certain comments that were made during my talk on love. If I could continue on with this, I would say that, basically, our relation to beauty is always one of love, because a relation of love goes beyond the simple pleasures of attraction or gratification. We all know what a pleasure it is to be with some people, especially if they are good-looking, friendly, or witty. But despite how plea-surable it may be, it still isn't love. We immediately know that love goes further than that and that it is also more demanding and more dangerous. This reminds me that, in my talk on love, I quoted an English philosopher from the eighteenth century, Hume, who says something wonderful. He says that a person's beauty has nothing to do with his or her features but is the consequence of his or her feeling desired. In this desire, which is directed toward the person for what he or she is, to what is absolutely mysterious and irreplaceable about him or her, I no longer know what or whom I love. That is what it is to love someone, to devote

oneself to someone who will always remain absolutely unknown. But through this very movement and because he
or she receives and feels this movement, the person relates
to him- or herself beyond him- or herself. And thus the
person is beautiful. Some romantic tales address this relationship between lovers, such as "Riquet with the Tuft" or
"Beauty and the Beast." The Beast is hideous, but when he
starts being loved by the Beauty in spite of and beyond his
ugliness, he turns into the marvelous prince we all know.

Q: Do you think we can live without beauty?

J-LN: Live, yes, we can always live poorly. I don't actually
think that anyone lives without beauty, but that doesn't
mean that everyone lives in relation to works of art, because not everyone has access to art. But I do think that
everyone has a sense of what we are talking about, solely
due to the fact of being a human being. We all know that
saying "it's beautiful" is not the same as saying "it's pretty,"
even if we are not always paying attention. It's enough to
point out that, in language, there is this difference between
the words. It would be interesting to see how the division
between *beautiful* and *pretty* is made in other languages.

To live without beauty is to live—as so often happens
in our lives—as a function of immediate needs or necessi-
ties. But every once in a while, we hear the call of beauty.
It is completely silent, but we do hear something.

For the last fifteen years or so, large exhibitions have
been attracting huge numbers of visitors. Recently there
were so many visitors for an exhibition at the Grand Palais—one that I didn't actually find all that successful—

that it stayed open for three nights in a row. A lot of people said that it was a sort of degradation of art reduced to a form of consumerism. One time they go to see Manet, another time they go to see Picasso or the pharaohs' treasure, and all of it together amounts to one large mass of cultural consumer goods. This is certainly true, but at the same time these thousands of people who go and may wait for a really long time just to see some art sense in some obscure way that they can't live without beauty. They do not really know what they are doing; they have been told over and over again that Monet, Cézanne, Picasso, and Delacroix were very important artists, and so they go to see them. But there'd be lots of good reasons for them to find the whole thing quite boring and to go see an entertaining movie instead. I am not saying that all the criticisms are false, but if so many people are visiting such exhibitions, something must be going on with this desire for beauty.

Q: But these people who go to see these exhibitions just because they've been told that they had to go there, will they then be in a position to recognize beauty? What bothers me is that they'll pass by something awe-inspiring in the street and won't even look at it.

J-LN: That doesn't bother me. We are too easily taken in by our society's constant self-criticism. What you are saying is true, but we can read it in all the magazines and so it doesn't really interest me. I prefer to tell myself that, among all these thousands of people, there are perhaps a few who'd do what you suspect they wouldn't. Because of seeing a Cézanne exhibition, the way they see might

119

change, and one day they might look differently at something they came across in the street. This is a wager—that much I'll grant you—but it is one I prefer to make, perhaps simply not to feel hopeless about everything. Perhaps it's better not to despair over everything.

Q (*from Gilberte T.*): Are there any more questions from children?

J-LN: Gilberte, you might point out that a child's question could also be posed by an adult who doesn't know he or she is posing a child's question.

Q: I'd like to know what, for you, is something that's not beautiful. But before I do that, I have a friend who'd like to say something.

   Mostly I'd just like to send greetings out to the whole of Val de Fontenay and to all the people who recognize me, Sofiane, Mohammed, Yanis, the whole "pink estate," *la cité rose*.

J-LN: Your greetings to the *cité rose* have been sent out. That's actually very interesting, because pink is suspended precisely between the pretty and the beautiful.

   You asked what, for me, isn't beautiful. I would say that it is one of two things: something that's not beautiful is completely withdrawn into the object and is purely functional. Such a thing is not beautiful, in the strict sense of the term. It's not ugly, either. There's an interesting category about which I had thought to say a word or two, one that could be symbolized by jewelry or extended to include all clothing. Jewelry, which is often described as beautiful, is on an order of beauty where it is always subordinated to something other than itself. The beauty of jewelry is made to accompany the presentation of a body or a piece of clothing. Jewelry alone is not of the same nature as a painting.

But now I'd like to introduce a third category. First, the category of the functional object, which isn't beautiful in the strict sense; then the category of jewelry, which is between beauty and being part of a functional ensemble; and then, the ugly. Ugliness is much more complicated, for it can also point toward the same thing as beauty does, but in its dark and terrible aspect. If beauty is unsettling, that is because it can open onto the terrible just as well as onto the sublime. Moreover, the word *sublime* can have two meanings. I didn't talk about that, either, because we didn't have enough time. Two very important authors have emphasized this relation of beauty to the terrible: one is Dostoyevsky, and the other is Rilke. Beauty is terrible; it is unsettling because it cannot be limited to suitability or harmony. It can enter into disharmony and dissonance; it can shatter all preferences, all suitability, and all agreements. The history of art clearly shows that we have constantly advanced by tearing up or destroying received conventions and beautiful forms. A century after Caravaggio, Poussin, a great French painter, said that Caravaggio came into the world to destroy painting. That's what Poussin thought of Caravaggio. You all know what could be said about Picasso and Cézanne, but also about Manet. This destruction of conventions, always begun anew throughout the history of art, tells us one thing: the sense of beauty cannot be satisfied with the sedimentation of forms in a harmony that gets repeated until it produces a classicism. From the moment that a form is simply repeated for its own sake, it no longer has anything to do with beauty. To awaken a sense of beauty, Rimbaud, who insulted beauty, says that destruction is necessary.

In this insult to beauty, the possibility of ugliness is also opened up. Since the nineteenth century, writings have appeared with *Aesthetic of Ugliness* in the title. I know of at least one work in German with that exact title.[1] With repulsive ugliness in the strong sense and not only in the functional one, the dark side is seen of what, in beauty, is seen from its bright side. Perhaps we can never really separate the two; for me, that is what Manet's *The Reading* represents. That is why ugliness can often be so fascinating.

Q: You said a while ago that beauty is universal and that each of us can recognize it, but do you think that the recognition of beauty can be learned through instruction [*par un apprentissage*]?

J-LN: Yes, of course. It is not simply given or self-evident, because often in an individual's development useful or functional forms are given priority. An individual can very easily grow up without ever being opened up to the universe of beauty—in fact, it is very frequently the case. It was my case until very late; I was more than twenty years old. I knew things about painting, but for me it was still only a big catalogue of images that belonged to humanity's culture of the West. I also have images of Chinese paintings, but the idea that it was a question of beauty in painting and in music had no real place in my universe. It's a question of one's milieu and one's preoccupations. So a kind of instruction or apprenticeship does exist, but one doesn't learn what's beautiful and what isn't. One learns that there is such a thing as art, that there are artists, art forms, music, and art history. One can show how each of these works can be approached, discerned, and, above all, that each of these works is inexhaustible. That's what a true education in beauty must do: show that certain creations, those of art, are inexhaustible, not because they are richer than other kinds, but because they are animated by a sense of the beyond or the infinite. One can learn that this exists and how it exists, and, through that learning process, one can accede to what, properly speaking, is not learned. This apprenticeship opens us up to this dimension, which perhaps we would never otherwise have reached. The certainty that this sense of beauty is present in us as human beings is what guided me in talking to you this evening, just as it also guided the great thinkers of beauty, Kant and Plato. This sense of beauty is present in a hidden or suppressed way, but it doesn't take much for someone, save perhaps those overwhelmed by misfortune and suffering, to be able to recognize that he or she knows something about it. Without this preliminary disposition, one couldn't learn anything, and I want to find this minimal disposition in the word *beautiful* and in the fact that we understand it to be different from *pretty*.

Q: A little while ago you said that, for you, there is no such thing as inner beauty, so how can you name it?

J-LN: No, it's not that inner beauty doesn't exist, but that the inner itself doesn't. I didn't say that inner beauty doesn't exist, but that this inner beauty has to be visible on the outside. So what I meant was that the inner doesn't exist; there is no inner. What we call the inner is that through which the outside is opened onto a beyond. But the opposition of the interior to the exterior doesn't mean anything. It is pure fantasy, the representation of a kind of phantom on the inside that would be the equivalent of the inner person as opposed to the external. That doesn't exist: on the inside, there is a skeleton and a stomach, not an immaterial soul. What is the soul? The great philosopher Aristotle tells us that the soul is the form of the body. So, if the body is beautiful, then the soul is beautiful, and vice versa, since it concerns the same thing. Imagine a really ugly or disgraced person being able to evince a beauty in his or her gesture, regard, intention, and also love, say, if he or she loves or is loved in excess of his or her appearance. That is when we would have to say that beauty is not in appearance but is in what shows through appearance and, quite possibly, despite appearance.

Q: You talk about beauty as if you were talking about god. I think they're both complete illusions. You only talked about the illusion of beauty.

J-LN: I will certainly grant you that god is an illusion according to a certain representation we make of these things. I would point out to you, however, that there is a very big difference between god and beauty. We represent god through the representation of a person, and from that moment onward, things go quite badly for god. But beauty is neither a person nor a thing. In sum, it is almost nothing at all.

(*Exchange continues.*) But in all of your really interesting and detailed explorations of beauty, there is nonetheless an impossibility of finding an absolute or a truth. I find that you talk about it in the same way as people talk about god.

J-LN: Indeed, perhaps I did talk about it as others might talk about god, as many great mystics in the great religions have talked about god and beauty. That's right.

(*Exchange continues.*) I would have preferred it if you had closed by saying that both this beauty and this god are illusions.

J-LN: But no, it's exactly the opposite. Of course, if you take any one of the paintings that I showed you, in a sense it has to do with an entire illusion machine.

(*Exchange continues.*) You're the one who is projecting an illusion, when you look at it.

J-LN: Not at all. It makes me see something other than the patches of color and the forms on the canvas, and this doesn't fall within the register of illusion at all. I see something else, and you do too, since you don't really seem like an iconoclast who would destroy all works of art.

(*Exchange continues.*) I make them.

J-LN: Okay, so you know very well that it's not about illusion.

(*Exchange continues.*) It is precisely because I make art that I am saying it involves an illusion.

J-LN: Hold on a minute, because I can see that we would have to have more dialogues, and not just dialogues for children, since this fellow is not very young anymore, even if he might not be as old as I am. We have to rid ourselves of this idea of illusion, which we always use whenever we want to say anything whatsoever. It serves our purposes, whether we're talking about a mirage or talking about god or talking about beauty, even when these things are not at all the same thing. An illusion is something that we're taken in by, whereas I have spent my time here today telling you that I cannot show beauty to you and that, particularly through works of art, beauty is what is shown in not being shown. There is nothing illusory in that. If you are convinced that what you do is illusory, then I hope you find another occupation.

(*Exchange continues.*) That doesn't necessarily follow.

J-LN: Then you must know it isn't all an illusion.

Q: I'd like to say something. I, who am handicapped, would like to say thank you to the children for their questions, because they've truly astonished me. These children have given my life direction this afternoon. When we say that truth comes out of the mouths of babes, therein lies the beauty of life entire.

J-LN: Thank you for saying so, because that's what we find too, at each one of these dialogues.

Notes

God

1. The astronomer in question was Daniel Kunth.

Justice

1. [Nancy is referring to the French political party La Droite libérale chrétienne, or the Liberal Christian Right.—Trans.]

Love

1. [*L'intime* can also refer to a close friend or to one who is most intimate to me.—Trans.]

2. If I had developed this parenthesis, I would have said roughly the following: to love oneself is not the same as egoism. It is necessary to love oneself. Indeed, it's dangerous not to love oneself and worse still to hate oneself. But just as with the love of another, we have to distinguish between loving a favorite object, preferring oneself over all others, which is egoism and in which I relate to myself as to a prized possession or to what I "have," and loving oneself in the very fact that one exists, that one "is" and in that sense, one is like any other, one has a unique "price," one counts in a unique way, for others as for oneself. In the former case, I love what is known and possessed, whereas in the latter,

I love the unknown. I love what I "am," the one who is always yet to be discovered and will also always remain unknown to me—who is receptive so that another may love him. Love always relates to the unknown or to the "mystery" of someone. And someone is always a mystery. (I come back to this issue further on, in response to one of the questions.)

3. To develop this idea, I would have insisted on the fact that the love children have for their parents is based on a relationship that is entirely dissymmetrical, since parents are there to protect and care for their children with a view to leading them toward autonomy and independence. This is not a love that wants to remain with the other person; on the contrary, it is one that wishes to detach itself from him or her, at the right moment and in the right way. The love of children for their parents responds to this protection and to this accompaniment, but it too is traversed by the movement of detaching. It does not want to be held back. It is like an inverse image of love, insofar as a mutual detachment is desired. Within love in the general sense, it is a matter of attachment—but nevertheless, this attachment also desires the autonomy of the other, desires that he or she be "him or herself," but without the dissymmetry brought about by protection and guidance.

4. I am adding something here that I didn't even mention while I was speaking as something that I had to leave by the wayside, since time was ticking away and I had to stop. According to my notes, I would have continued to say that this fidelity to commitment is not solely a matter of feelings or desire. Feelings and desires have a life of their own. They can come and go, disappear and reappear, can be directed toward others as well as toward him or her to whom one is committed. This can lead sometimes to a breakup, which is often the least terrible outcome. But it can also lead to a greater clarity regarding where one's commitment lies, to a greater recognition both of the other person in his or her uniqueness and singularity and of how my engagement constitutes a part of this singularity.

5. I thought it might be interesting to indicate whether the question was posed by a girl [G] or a boy [B]. In places where there is no such indication, it is because an exchange continued with the same person.

6. After reading the transcription of this answer, I wanted to correct myself. This is not the only sense of love. The sense of love is also,

and even necessarily, beyond all expectation of return. It is primarily a nonexpectation or a beyond of expectation: "I want that you be," as Augustine says. And we know that there is such a thing as unreciprocated love. What I would say is that there is doubtless always a return in the very fact of demonstrating love, in the transport or in the disposition with which it affects me. Love on its own is pleasing to itself or in itself. But what pleases in that way is, again, something that comes from outside, if not precisely from the other person to whom it is directed. In reading the next question and answer, I see that we were already heading in that direction.

7. [The definition of beauty to which Nancy refers can be found in Voltaire's *Philosophical Dictionary* of 1764.—Trans.]

Beauty

1. [*Aesthetic of Ugliness* (*Aesthetik des Hässlichen*) is a book by German philosopher Karl Rosencrantz, written in 1863.—Trans.]